GO!

Ethics in Cyberspace

First Edition

Alan Evans

PRENTICE HALL

Upper Saddle River, New Jersey
Columbus, Ohio

Library of Congress Cataloging-in-Publication Data

Evans, Alan (Alan D.)
  Ethics in cyberspace / Alan Evans. — 1st ed.
      p. cm.
  At head of title: Go!
  Includes index.
  ISBN-13: 978-0-13-505293-8
  ISBN-10: 0-13-505293-9
  1. Computers—Moral and ethical aspects.   2. Internet—Moral and ethical aspects.   I. Title.   II. Title: Go!

QA76.9.M65E93 2009
303.48'34—dc22

2008054006

VP/Editorial Director: Natalie E. Anderson
Editor in Chief: Michael Payne
Associate VP/Executive Acquisitions Editor, Print:
  Stephanie Wall
Director, Product Development: Pamela Hersperger
Product Development Manager: Eileen Bien Calabro
Editorial Project Manager: Laura Burgess
Development Editor: Ginny Bess Munroe
Editorial Assistant: Terenia McHenry
AVP/Executive Editor, Media: Richard Keaveny
AVP/Director of Product Development: Lisa Strite
Editorial Media Project Manager: Alana Coles
Production Media Project Manager: John Cassar
Director of Marketing: Kate Valentine
Marketing Manager: Tori Olson Alves
Marketing Assistant: Angela Frey
Marketing Coordinator: Susan Osterlitz
Senior Managing Editor: Cynthia Zonneveld
Associate Managing Editor: Camille Trentacoste
Production Project Manager: Mike Lackey
Manager of Rights & Permissions: Charles Morris

Senior Operations Specialist: Nick Sklitsis
Operations Specialist: Natacha Moore
Senior Art Director: Jonathan Boylan
Art Director: Anthony Gemmellaro
Cover Illustration/Photo: Courtesy of Getty Images, Inc./
  Marvin Mattelson
Director, Image Resource Center: Melinda Patelli
Manager, Rights and Permissions: Zina Arabia
Manager: Visual Research: Beth Brenzel
Manager, Cover Visual Research & Permissions: Karen
  Sanatar
Image Permission Coordinator: Cynthia Vincenti
Photo Researcher: Sheila Norman
Composition: GGS Higher Education Resources, A
  Division of Premedia Global, Inc.
Full-Service Project Management: GGS Higher Education
  Resources, A Division of Premedia Global, Inc.
Printer/Binder: R.R. Donnelley/Menasha
Cover Printer: Lehigh-Phoenix Color/Hagerstown
Typeface: Bookman

Microsoft, Windows, Word, Microsoft, Windows, Word, PowerPoint, Outlook, FrontPage, Visual Basic, MSN, The Microsoft Network, and/or other Microsoft products referenced herein are either trademarks or registered trademarks of the Microsoft Corporation in the U.S.A. and other countries. Screen shots and icons reprinted with permission from the Microsoft Corporation. This book is not sponsored or endorsed by or affiliated with the Microsoft Corporation.

The information contained in *Ethics in Cyberspace* is of broad general usefulness to the reader. This publication is sold with the understanding that the publisher and the author are **not** rendering legal or other professional services or advice. The information contained in this publication is intended to serve educational purposes and is **not** a substitute for the advice of a competent professional, legal or otherwise. The author and the publisher each make no warranty of any kind, express or implied, with regard to this book, or the accuracy or timeliness of its content. Any use of or reliance upon this book is at the reader's own risk, and the author and the publisher specifically disclaim any liability resulting directly or indirectly from the use, reliance or application of any of the content of this book.

Credits and acknowledgments borrowed from other sources and reproduced, with permission, in this textbook appear at the end of this front matter.

Pearson Education Ltd., London
Pearson Education Singapore, Pte. Ltd
Pearson Education, Canada, Inc.
Pearson Education–Japan
Pearson Education Australia PTY, Limited

Pearson Education North Asia Ltd., Hong Kong
Pearson Educación de Mexico, S.A. de C.V.
Pearson Education Malaysia, Pte. Ltd.
Pearson Education, Upper Saddle River, New Jersey

Prentice Hall
is an imprint of

www.pearsonhighered.com

9 8 7 6 5 4 3 2 1
ISBN-13: 978-0-13-505293-8
ISBN-10: 0-13-505293-9

Table of Contents

Letter from the Editor

Dear Instructors and Students,

The primary goal of the *GO!* Series is two-fold. The first goal is to help instructors teach the course they want in less time. The second goal is to provide students with the skills to solve business problems using the computer as a tool, for both themselves and the organization for which they might be employed.

The *GO!* Series was originally created by Series Editor Shelley Gaskin and published with the release of Microsoft Office 2003. Her ideas came from years of using textbooks that didn't meet all the needs of today's diverse classroom and that were too confusing for students. Shelley continues to enhance the series by ensuring we stay true to our vision of developing quality instruction and useful classroom tools.

But we also need your input and ideas.

Over time, the *GO!* Series has evolved based on direct feedback from instructors and students using the series. *We are the publisher that listens.* To publish a textbook that works for you, it's critical that we continue to listen to this feedback. It's important to me to talk with you and hear your stories about using *GO!* Your voice can make a difference.

My hope is that this letter will inspire you to write me an e-mail and share your thoughts on using the *GO!* Series.

Stephanie Wall
Executive Editor, *GO!* Series
stephanie_wall@prenhall.com

GO! System Contributors

We thank the following people for their hard work and support in making the *GO!* System all that it is!

Additional Author Support

Bell, Susan	Mendocino College
Coyle, Diane	Montgomery County Community College
Fry, Susan	Boise State
Townsend, Kris	Spokane Falls Community College
Stroup, Tracey	Amgen Corporation

Instructor Resource Authors

Amer, Beverly	Northern Arizona University	Paterson, Jim	Paradise Valley Community College
Boito, Nancy	Harrisburg Area Community College	Prince, Lisa	Missouri State
Coyle, Diane	Montgomery County Community College	Rodgers, Gwen	Southern Nazarene University
Dawson, Tamara	Southern Nazarene University	Ruymann, Amy	Burlington Community College
Driskel, Loretta	Niagara County Community College	Ryan, Bob	Montgomery County Community College
Elliott, Melissa	Odessa College		
Fry, Susan	Boise State	Smith, Diane	Henry Ford Community College
Geoghan, Debra	Bucks County Community College	Spangler, Candice	Columbus State Community College
Hearn, Barbara	Community College of Philadelphia	Thompson, Joyce	Lehigh Carbon Community College
Jones, Stephanie	South Plains College	Tiffany, Janine	Reading Area Community College
Madsen, Donna	Kirkwood Community College	Watt, Adrienne	Douglas College
Meck, Kari	Harrisburg Area Community College	Weaver, Paul	Bossier Parish Community College
Miller, Cindy	Ivy Tech	Weber, Sandy	Gateway Technical College
Nowakowski, Tony	Buffalo State	Wood, Dawn	
Pace, Phyllis	Queensborough Community College	Weissman, Jonathan	Finger Lakes Community College

Super Reviewers

Brotherton, Cathy	Riverside Community College	Maurer, Trina	Odessa College
Cates, Wally	Central New Mexico Community College	Meck, Kari	Harrisburg Area Community College
		Miller, Cindy	Ivy Tech Community College
Cone, Bill	Northern Arizona University	Nielson, Phil	Salt Lake Community College
Coverdale, John	Riverside Community College	Rodgers, Gwen	Southern Nazarene University
Foster, Nancy	Baker College	Smolenski, Robert	Delaware Community College
Helfand, Terri	Chaffey College	Spangler, Candice	Columbus State Community College
Hibbert, Marilyn	Salt Lake Community College	Thompson, Joyce	Lehigh Carbon Community College
Holliday, Mardi	Community College of Philadelphia	Weber, Sandy	Gateway Technical College
Jerry, Gina	Santa Monica College	Wells, Lorna	Salt Lake Community College
Martin, Carol	Harrisburg Area Community College	Zaboski, Maureen	University of Scranton

Technical Editors

Janice Snyder
Joyce Nielsen
Colette Eisele
Janet Pickard
Mara Zebest
Lindsey Allen
William Daley
LeeAnn Bates

Student Reviewers

Allen, John	Asheville-Buncombe Tech Community College	Erickson, Mike	Ball State University
		Gadomski, Amanda	Northern Michigan University
Alexander, Steven	St. Johns River Community College	Gyselinck, Craig	Central Washington University
Alexander, Melissa	Tulsa Community College	Harrison, Margo	Central Washington University
Bolz, Stephanie	Northern Michigan University	Heacox, Kate	Central Washington University
Berner, Ashley	Central Washington University	Hill, Cheretta	Northwestern State University
Boomer, Michelle	Northern Michigan University	Innis, Tim	Tulsa Community College
Busse, Brennan	Northern Michigan University	Jarboe, Aaron	Central Washington University
Butkey, Maura	Central Washington University	Klein, Colleen	Northern Michigan University
Christensen, Kaylie	Northern Michigan University	Moeller, Jeffrey	Northern Michigan University
Connally, Brianna	Central Washington University	Nicholson, Regina	Athens Tech College
Davis, Brandon	Northern Michigan University	Niehaus, Kristina	Northern Michigan University
Davis, Christen	Central Washington University	Nisa, Zaibun	Santa Rosa Community College
Den Boer, Lance	Central Washington University	Nunez, Nohelia	Santa Rosa Community College
Dix, Jessica	Central Washington University	Oak, Samantha	Central Washington University
Moeller, Jeffrey	Northern Michigan University	Oertii, Monica	Central Washington University
Downs, Elizabeth	Central Washington University	Palenshus, Juliet	Central Washington University

Pohl, Amanda	Northern Michigan University	Shanahan, Megan	Northern Michigan University
Presnell, Randy	Central Washington University	Teska, Erika	Hawaii Pacific University
Ritner, April	Northern Michigan University	Traub, Amy	Northern Michigan University
Rodriguez, Flavia	Northwestern State University	Underwood, Katie	Central Washington University
Roberts, Corey	Tulsa Community College	Walters, Kim	Central Washington University
Rossi, Jessica Ann	Central Washington University	Wilson, Kelsie	Central Washington University
Shafapay, Natasha	Central Washington University	Wilson, Amanda	Green River Community College

Series Reviewers

Abraham, Reni	Houston Community College	Crawford, Thomasina	Miami-Dade College, Kendall Campus
Agatston, Ann	Agatston Consulting Technical College	Credico, Grace	Lethbridge Community College
		Crenshaw, Richard	Miami Dade Community College, North
Alexander, Melody	Ball Sate University		
Alejandro, Manuel	Southwest Texas Junior College	Crespo, Beverly	Mt. San Antonio College
Ali, Farha	Lander University	Crossley, Connie	Cincinnati State Technical Community College
Amici, Penny	Harrisburg Area Community College		
Anderson, Patty A.	Lake City Community College	Curik, Mary	Central New Mexico Community College
Andrews, Wilma	Virginia Commonwealth College, Nebraska University		
		De Arazoza, Ralph	Miami Dade Community College
Anik, Mazhar	Tiffin University	Danno, John	DeVry University/Keller Graduate School
Armstrong, Gary	Shippensburg University		
Atkins, Bonnie	Delaware Technical Community College	Davis, Phillip	Del Mar College
		DeHerrera, Laurie	Pikes Peak Community College
Bachand, LaDonna	Santa Rosa Community College	Delk, Dr. K. Kay	Seminole Community College
Bagui, Sikha	University of West Florida	Doroshow, Mike	Eastfield College
Beecroft, Anita	Kwantlen University College	Douglas, Gretchen	SUNYCortland
Bell, Paula	Lock Haven College	Dove, Carol	Community College of Allegheny
Belton, Linda	Springfield Tech. Community College	Driskel, Loretta	Niagara Community College
		Duckwiler, Carol	Wabaunsee Community College
Bennett, Judith	Sam Houston State University	Duncan, Mimi	University of Missouri-St. Louis
Bhatia, Sai	Riverside Community College	Duthie, Judy	Green River Community College
Bishop, Frances	DeVry Institute—Alpharetta (ATL)	Duvall, Annette	Central New Mexico Community College
Blaszkiewicz, Holly	Ivy Tech Community College/Region 1		
Branigan, Dave	DeVry University	Ecklund, Paula	Duke University
Bray, Patricia	Allegany College of Maryland	Eng, Bernice	Brookdale Community College
Brotherton, Cathy	Riverside Community College	Evans, Billie	Vance-Granville Community College
Buehler, Lesley	Ohlone College	Feuerbach, Lisa	Ivy Tech East Chicago
Buell, C	Central Oregon Community College	Fisher, Fred	Florida State University
Byars, Pat	Brookhaven College	Foster, Penny L.	Anne Arundel Community College
Byrd, Lynn	Delta State University, Cleveland, Mississippi	Foszcz, Russ	McHenry County College
		Fry, Susan	Boise State University
Cacace, Richard N.	Pensacola Junior College	Fustos, Janos	Metro State
Cadenhead, Charles	Brookhaven College	Gallup, Jeanette	Blinn College
Calhoun, Ric	Gordon College	Gelb, Janet	Grossmont College
Cameron, Eric	Passaic Community College	Gentry, Barb	Parkland College
Carriker, Sandra	North Shore Community College	Gerace, Karin	St. Angela Merici School
Cannamore, Madie	Kennedy King	Gerace, Tom	Tulane University
Carreon, Cleda	Indiana University—Purdue University, Indianapolis	Ghajar, Homa	Oklahoma State University
		Gifford, Steve	Northwest Iowa Community College
Chaffin, Catherine	Shawnee State University	Glazer, Ellen	Broward Community College
Chauvin, Marg	Palm Beach Community College, Boca Raton	Gordon, Robert	Hofstra University
		Gramlich, Steven	Pasco-Hernando Community College
Challa, Chandrashekar	Virginia State University	Graviett, Nancy M.	St. Charles Community College, St. Peters, Missouri
Chamlou, Afsaneh	NOVA Alexandria		
Chapman, Pam	Wabaunsee Community College	Greene, Rich	Community College of Allegheny County
Christensen, Dan	Iowa Western Community College		
Clay, Betty	Southeastern Oklahoma State University	Gregoryk, Kerry	Virginia Commonwealth State
		Griggs, Debra	Bellevue Community College
Collins, Linda D.	Mesa Community College	Grimm, Carol	Palm Beach Community College
Conroy-Link, Janet	Holy Family College	Hahn, Norm	Thomas Nelson Community College
Cosgrove, Janet	Northwestern CT Community	Hammerschlag, Dr. Bill	Brookhaven College
Courtney, Kevin	Hillsborough Community College	Hansen, Michelle	Davenport University
Cox, Rollie	Madison Area Technical College	Hayden, Nancy	Indiana University—Purdue University, Indianapolis
Crawford, Hiram	Olive Harvey College		

Hayes, Theresa	Broward Community College	Lord, Alexandria	Asheville Buncombe Tech
Helfand, Terri	Chaffey College	Lowe, Rita	Harold Washington College
Helms, Liz	Columbus State Community College	Low, Willy Hui	Joliet Junior College
Hernandez, Leticia	TCI College of Technology	Lucas, Vickie	Broward Community College
Hibbert, Marilyn	Salt Lake Community College	Lynam, Linda	Central Missouri State University
Hoffman, Joan	Milwaukee Area Technical College	Lyon, Lynne	Durham College
Hogan, Pat	Cape Fear Community College	Lyon, Pat Rajski	Tomball College
Holland, Susan	Southeast Community College	MacKinnon, Ruth	Georgia Southern University
Hopson, Bonnie	Athens Technical College	Macon, Lisa	Valencia Community College, West
Horvath, Carrie	Albertus Magnus College		Campus
Horwitz, Steve	Community College of Philadelphia	Machuca, Wayne	College of the Sequoias
Hotta, Barbara	Leeward Community College	Madison, Dana	Clarion University
Howard, Bunny	St. Johns River Community	Maguire, Trish	Eastern New Mexico University
Howard, Chris	DeVry University	Malkan, Rajiv	Montgomery College
Huckabay, Jamie	Austin Community College	Manning, David	Northern Kentucky University
Hudgins, Susan	East Central University	Marcus, Jacquie	Niagara Community College
Hulett, Michelle J.	Missouri State University	Marghitu, Daniela	Auburn University
Hunt, Darla A.	Morehead State University,	Marks, Suzanne	Bellevue Community College
	Morehead, Kentucky	Marquez, Juanita	El Centro College
Hunt, Laura	Tulsa Community College	Marquez, Juan	Mesa Community College
Jacob, Sherry	Jefferson Community College	Martyn, Margie	Baldwin-Wallace College
Jacobs, Duane	Salt Lake Community College	Marucco, Toni	Lincoln Land Community College
Jauken, Barb	Southeastern Community	Mason, Lynn	Lubbock Christian University
Johnson, Kathy	Wright College	Matutis, Audrone	Houston Community College
Johnson, Mary	Kingwood College	Matkin, Marie	University of Lethbridge
Johnson, Mary	Mt. San Antonio College	McCain, Evelynn	Boise State University
Jones, Stacey	Benedict College	McCannon, Melinda	Gordon College
Jones, Warren	University of Alabama, Birmingham	McCarthy, Marguerite	Northwestern Business College
Jordan, Cheryl	San Juan College	McCaskill, Matt L.	Brevard Community College
Kapoor, Bhushan	California State University, Fullerton	McClellan, Carolyn	Tidewater Community College
Kasai, Susumu	Salt Lake Community College	McClure, Darlean	College of Sequoias
Kates, Hazel	Miami Dade Community College,	McCrory, Sue A.	Missouri State University
	Kendall	McCue, Stacy	Harrisburg Area Community College
Keen, Debby	University of Kentucky	McEntire-Orbach, Teresa	Middlesex County College
Keeter, Sandy	Seminole Community College	McLeod, Todd	Fresno City College
Kern-Blystone,		McManus, Illyana	Grossmont College
Dorothy Jean	Bowling Green State	McPherson, Dori	Schoolcraft College
Keskin, Ilknur	The University of South Dakota	Meiklejohn, Nancy	Pikes Peak Community College
Kirk, Colleen	Mercy College	Menking, Rick	Hardin-Simmons University
Kleckner, Michelle	Elon University	Meredith, Mary	University of Louisiana at Lafayette
Kliston, Linda	Broward Community College, North	Mermelstein, Lisa	Baruch College
	Campus	Metos, Linda	Salt Lake Community College
Kochis, Dennis	Suffolk County Community College	Meurer, Daniel	University of Cincinnati
Kramer, Ed	Northern Virginia Community	Meyer, Marian	Central New Mexico Community
	College		College
Laird, Jeff	Northeast State Community College	Miller, Cindy	Ivy Tech Community College,
Lamoureaux, Jackie	Central New Mexico Community		Lafayette, Indiana
	College	Mitchell, Susan	Davenport University
Lange, David	Grand Valley State	Mohle, Dennis	Fresno Community College
LaPointe, Deb	Central New Mexico Community	Monk, Ellen	University of Delaware
	College	Moore, Rodney	Holland College
Larson, Donna	Louisville Technical Institute	Morris, Mike	Southeastern Oklahoma State
Laspina, Kathy	Vance-Granville Community College		University
Le Grand, Dr. Kate	Broward Community College	Morris, Nancy	Hudson Valley Community College
Lenhart, Sheryl	Terra Community College	Moseler, Dan	Harrisburg Area Community College
Letavec, Chris	University of Cincinnati	Nabors, Brent	Reedley College, Clovis Center
Liefert, Jane	Everett Community College	Nadas, Erika	Wright College
Lindaman, Linda	Black Hawk Community College	Nadelman, Cindi	New England College
Lindberg, Martha	Minnesota State University	Nademlynsky, Lisa	Johnson & Wales University
Lightner, Renee	Broward Community College	Ncube, Cathy	University of West Florida
Lindberg, Martha	Minnesota State University	Nagengast, Joseph	Florida Career College
Linge, Richard	Arizona Western College	Newsome, Eloise	Northern Virginia Community
Logan, Mary G.	Delgado Community College		College Woodbridge
Loizeaux, Barbara	Westchester Community College	Nicholls, Doreen	Mohawk Valley Community College
Lopez, Don	Clovis-State Center Community	Nunan, Karen	Northeast State Technical
	College District		Community College

Odegard, Teri — Edmonds Community College
Ogle, Gregory — North Community College
Orr, Dr. Claudia — Northern Michigan University South
Otieno, Derek — DeVry University
Otton, Diana Hill — Chesapeake College
Oxendale, Lucia — West Virginia Institute of Technology

Paiano, Frank — Southwestern College
Patrick, Tanya — Clackamas Community College
Peairs, Deb — Clark State Community College
Prince, Lisa — Missouri State University-Springfield Campus
Proietti, Kathleen — Northern Essex Community College
Pusins, Delores — HCCC
Raghuraman, Ram — Joliet Junior College
Reasoner, Ted Allen — Indiana University—Purdue
Reeves, Karen — High Point University
Remillard, Debbie — New Hampshire Technical Institute
Rhue, Shelly — DeVry University
Richards, Karen — Maplewoods Community College
Richardson, Mary — Albany Technical College
Rodgers, Gwen — Southern Nazarene University
Roselli, Diane — Harrisburg Area Community College
Ross, Dianne — University of Louisiana in Lafayette
Rousseau, Mary — Broward Community College, South
Samson, Dolly — Hawaii Pacific University
Sams, Todd — University of Cincinnati
Sandoval, Everett — Reedley College
Sardone, Nancy — Seton Hall University
Scafide, Jean — Mississippi Gulf Coast Community College
Scheeren, Judy — Westmoreland County Community College
Schneider, Sol — Sam Houston State University
Scroggins, Michael — Southwest Missouri State University
Sever, Suzanne — Northwest Arkansas Community College
Sheridan, Rick — California State University-Chico
Silvers, Pamela — Asheville Buncombe Tech
Singer, Steven A. — University of Hawai'i, Kapi'olani Community College
Sinha, Atin — Albany State University
Skolnick, Martin — Florida Atlantic University
Smith, T. Michael — Austin Community College
Smith, Tammy — Tompkins Cortland Community Collge
Smolenski, Bob — Delaware County Community College
Spangler, Candice — Columbus State
Stedham, Vicki — St. Petersburg College, Clearwater
Stefanelli, Greg — Carroll Community College
Steiner, Ester — New Mexico State University
Stenlund, Neal — Northern Virginia Community College, Alexandria
St. John, Steve — Tulsa Community College

Sterling, Janet — Houston Community College
Stoughton, Catherine — Laramie County Community College
Sullivan, Angela — Joliet Junior College
Szurek, Joseph — University of Pittsburgh at Greensburg
Tarver, Mary Beth — Northwestern State University
Taylor, Michael — Seattle Central Community College
Thangiah, Sam — Slippery Rock University
Thompson-Sellers, Ingrid — Georgia Perimeter College
Tomasi, Erik — Baruch College
Toreson, Karen — Shoreline Community College
Trifiletti, John J. — Florida Community College at Jacksonville
Trivedi, Charulata — Quinsigamond Community College, Woodbridge
Tucker, William — Austin Community College
Turgeon, Cheryl — Asnuntuck Community College
Turpen, Linda — Central New Mexico Community College
Upshaw, Susan — Del Mar College
Unruh, Angela — Central Washington University
Vanderhoof, Dr. Glenna — Missouri State University-Springfield Campus
Vargas, Tony — El Paso Community College
Vicars, Mitzi — Hampton University
Villarreal, Kathleen — Fresno
Vitrano, Mary Ellen — Palm Beach Community College
Volker, Bonita — Tidewater Community College
Wahila, Lori (Mindy) — Tompkins Cortland Community College
Waswick, Kim — Southeast Community College, Nebraska
Wavle, Sharon — Tompkins Cortland Community College
Webb, Nancy — City College of San Francisco
Wells, Barbara E. — Central Carolina Technical College
Wells, Lorna — Salt Lake Community College
Welsh, Jean — Lansing Community College Nebraska
White, Bruce — Quinnipiac University
Willer, Ann — Solano Community College
Williams, Mark — Lane Community College
Wilson, Kit — Red River College
Wilson, Roger — Fairmont State University
Wimberly, Leanne — International Academy of Design and Technology
Worthington, Paula — Northern Virginia Community College
Yauney, Annette — Herkimer County Community College
Yip, Thomas — Passaic Community College
Zavala, Ben — Webster Tech
Zlotow, Mary Ann — College of DuPage
Zudeck, Steve — Broward Community College, North

About the Author

Alan Evans is currently a faculty member at Manor College and Montgomery County Community College teaching a variety of computer science and business courses. He holds a B.S. in Accounting from Rider University and an M.S. in Information Systems from Drexel University as well as being a Certified Public Accountant. After a successful career in business, Alan finally realized his true calling was education. He has been teaching at the college level since 2000. Alan enjoys giving presentations at technical conferences and meets regularly with computer science faculty and administrators from other colleges to discuss curriculum development and new methods of engaging students.

Credits

1 chapter**one**

Computer Ethics, Copyright, and Plagiarism

OBJECTIVES

At the end of this chapter you will be able to:

1. Define Ethics, Systems of Personal Ethics, and Personal Ethics

2. Determine How to Make Ethical Choices

3. Decide Which Ethical Guidelines to Follow

4. Define Intellectual Property and Copyright

5. Understand Permissible Use of Copyrighted Material

6. Describe Copyright Infringement

7. Explain the Consequences of Copyright Infringement and How to Avoid Infringement

8. Define Fair Use

9. Explain How to Protect Your Work Against Infringement

10. Define Plagiarism

Introduction

The Internet has changed the way the world works. Now you can easily order merchandise from online merchants or auction sites with a few clicks of the mouse. Information is readily available on almost any imaginable topic, and most of the time, the information is accessible free of charge. In addition, with social networking tools like MySpace and Facebook, you can easily set up a profile of yourself and your interests and you can connect with your friends across cyberspace. Life is more convenient with the Internet!

However, what happens when you buy a product on the Internet, such as on eBay, and it doesn't arrive? What if the seller disappears with your money? Or, what if you receive a failing grade on your latest research paper for your history class because the Web sites you used for source material were inaccurate? Finally, what if you read rumors on MySpace about getting fired from your last job for shoplifting, and the rumor is completely untrue? Unfortunately, not everyone on the Internet is your friend, and many people behave unethically.

In this chapter, you will explore some of the ethical issues that you will encounter online, and you will learn strategies for detecting unethical behavior and protecting yourself from less scrupulous individuals. First, you will explore what ethics are and where they come from.

Objective 1
Define Ethics, Systems of Ethical Conduct, and Personal Ethics

What are ethics? *Ethics* is the study of the general nature of morals and of the specific moral choices made by individuals. Ethics are the guidelines you use to make decisions each day. For example, if you are standing in line at a convenience store and you see someone drop a dollar, the decision that you make about whether you tap the person on the shoulder and tell him about it or pick up and keep the dollar is an ethical choice you must make.

Does everyone have the same ethical values? Ethics vary widely from country to country and person to person. For example, in Western cultures (especially in America), privacy or secrecy is viewed as an inalienable right. However, in many Eastern cultures, people are perceived as having something to hide if they behave in a secretive manner. Every culture has its own unique system of ethical conduct. In this chapter, you will explore a few of the more common ethical systems.

In what types of ethical systems do individuals make their own decisions? *Relativism* is a theory in which there are no universal definitions of right and wrong; it is the individual's decision about how to act. With this system, individuals or groups of people can have completely opposing opinions about an ethical issue, and neither side is wrong. There are two relativism philosophies—subjective relativism and cultural relativism.

What is subjective relativism? With *subjective relativism*, each individual decides for himself what is right and wrong, and therefore, no one's views are more valid than anyone else's. This may seem like an ideal theory, but it doesn't work well in the real world. If everyone can just make their own decisions about right and wrong, then we would have a rather chaotic world. Consider if everyone could choose whether stealing from others is acceptable. You may feel that stealing is unethical, whereas the person next to you feels there is no problem with relieving a weaker individual of his property. You would never know when you could feel safe with your possessions and would constantly be worrying about some less ethical person stealing the lunch you just purchased.

What is cultural relativism? *Cultural relativism* means that right and wrong are defined by the accepted moral code of a society at a given place and in a given point in time (attitudes can change). For instance, in the United States, it is normally accepted that you will wear clothing (or at least cover certain strategic areas) when going out in public. Cultural relativism usually works better in practice if the alternative is leaving moral decisions up to individuals with no guidelines (as subjective relativists would).

Do some ethical values vary depending on the situation? Another ethical philosophy is *situational ethics*. The situational ethics theory, developed by American professor Joseph Fletcher, says that decision making should be based on the circumstances of a particular situation and not on fixed laws. Fletcher believed that other moral principles can be ignored to follow the overriding principle of love (meaning unconditional love for all people). This type of ethical system, because it depends solely on an individual's interpretation of what will increase love, is probably not ideal in a real-world setting either. Some people do change their values based on the situation, often for convenience. For example, a person might feel that stealing is wrong, but when he needs a ream of paper for his home laser printer, he may take it out of the supply closet at work because he doesn't have time to go to the office supply store. This is not an example of situational ethics as defined by Fletcher, but rather a case of a person with "flexible" ethics.

Are laws passed to guide people's ethical actions? *Rule utilitarianism* is an ethical theory that espouses establishing moral guidelines through specific rules (or laws). The idea behind this system is that if everyone adheres to the same moral code, society as a whole will improve and people will be happier. Many societies follow this system in general terms, including the United States.

Do religions influence ethics? Some ethical systems are based on religious traditions. For example, the expression *Judeo-Christian ethics* refers to the common set of basic values shared between Jewish and Christian religious traditions. These include behaviors like respecting property rights, treating others with kindness, respecting elders, and not interfering with other people's personal relationships.

Are there people who have no ethics? Everyone has a system of ethics to which they adhere. You may not agree with someone's ethical choices, but that doesn't mean they don't possess ethics. However, sometimes people act in a manner that violates the beliefs of the group or the geographical area in which they live. *Unethical behavior* means not conforming to a set of approved standards of social or professional behavior. This is different than *amoral behavior*, which is when a person does not know what is right or wrong and has no interest in the moral consequences of his actions.

Is unethical behavior a euphemism for illegal activity? Unethical behavior does not have to be illegal. *Laws* are groups of rules and principles that direct actions within a community. Laws are enforced by government agencies (such as the police, the Federal Bureau of Investigation, the Food and Drug Administration, and so on) and interpreted by the courts. It is not possible to pass laws that cover every potential behavior that human beings can engage in. Therefore, *societal ethics* provide a general set of unwritten guidelines for people to live by. However, as the interpretation of ethics varies from person to person, ethics are difficult and even impossible to enforce, and just because an action isn't illegal doesn't mean that it isn't unethical.

An example of an unethical but not illegal practice is supermarket slotting fees. These are fees that some supermarkets charge to produce companies and product manufacturers for the privilege of having their products placed on their store shelves. This is considered unethical by many people because it puts smaller companies at a disadvantage. Most smaller companies cannot afford to pay the fees. It is difficult to prove your product will sell to consumers if you cannot get it on to store shelves. Ice cream company owners Ben and Jerry faced this daunting problem when they first tried to get chain grocery stores to carry their fledgling products.

Which system of ethics works best? There is no clear superior choice among ethics systems. Most societies use a blend of the different systems. Regardless of the ethical system of the society in which you live, all ethical decisions are greatly influenced by personal ethics.

What are personal ethics? Every day you undertake specific actions and make statements to others. You make decisions about how to behave based on a set of criteria. Maybe you strive to be as happy as you possibly can be or maybe you try to ensure that others around you are safe and secure. Perhaps you are seeking to eliminate a source of discomfort or conflict in your life. Most likely, your words and actions are predicated on a combination of various goals. To select these words and actions, you follow a set of ***personal ethics***, which is a set of criteria by which you make decisions that affect your personal life. Many people have well-defined principles they follow on a consistent basis. Other people behave less consistently and may not choose the same actions for a similar situation. Each person's personal ethics are unique to himself.

Your personal ethics may dictate that lying is inappropriate. But sometimes pressure to avoid unpleasant consequences may cause you to adjust this principle, and you may lie as a result. For instance, if you are applying for a job with an employer that you know has a high pay scale, you might consider exaggerating how much you are making at your current job in an attempt to gain a higher starting salary. Is an exaggeration a lie? Is it justified behavior to avoid being underpaid? You know you are worth a higher salary and will work hard for the company if it gives you the job. On the other hand, if you tell the truth, you may start at a lower salary making it tougher in the short term to maintain your lifestyle. The consequences of lying on most job applications can result in termination if you are caught. Weighing all these complex factors and deciding on a course of action is an ethical decision.

How do a person's ethics develop? There are many contributors to our ethical development, as Figure 1.1 illustrates. You may have thought about some of these factors, but others may have influenced you without your conscious knowledge. Surely, your family has a major impact on establishing the values you cherish in your life. You may also have a cultural bias toward certain moral positions.

Your religious affiliation is another major factor in the development of your ethical life. Most religions have established specific codes of ethical conduct. How these sets of ethics interact with the values of the larger culture is often challenging. Issues such as abortion, the use of the death penalty, and a country's involvement in war all can cause conflict between people's personal ethical systems and the established legal and societal ethics systems.

As you mature, your life experiences will offer you opportunity to develop your personal ethics. Does the behavior you see around you make sense within the ethical systems of your family, your church, or your educational institution? Has your experience led you to abandon some ethical rules and adopt others? Have you modified how and when you apply these laws of conduct depending on what is at stake?

Finally, your daily life experiences influence your personal ethics. How well did things work out with the last ethical decision you made? If your decision was accepted by your family, peers, and society at large, you will likely make the same decision again under similar circumstances. Conversely, if you received criticism or a penalty for your actions, this might cause you to alter your ethical code in the future. Also, as you face decisions with higher stakes (changing jobs, getting married, and buying a home), the ethical framework you make decisions in may tend to shift.

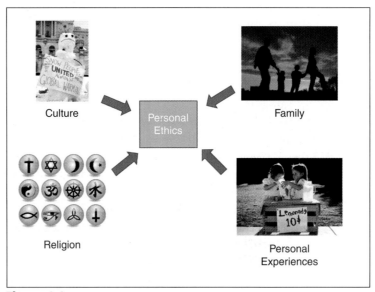

Figure 1.1
Many influences affect the development of your personal ethics.

Objective 2
Determine How to Make Ethical Choices

Do all decisions involve an ethical component? Not all choices require an ethical evaluation. For instance, if you buy a new iPod, you might choose green from the available color choices. The decision to choose green is a personal preference and doesn't involve an ethical decision.

Ethical choices involve **voluntary actions**—not situations where you react instinctively or are coerced. Suppose you see a toddler crossing the street and you notice a speeding car careening toward the child. You leap into the street and knock the toddler out of the path of the car, but you land on the child and break his leg. Yes, you harmed another human being—which is usually considered unethical—but you reacted by reflex in a scary situation. Therefore, you did not make an unethical decision even if your actions lead to harming a child.

What important points do you need to consider when making ethical choices? Each person has his or her own system of analyzing a situation and then applying personal ethics to that situation. However, asking three questions before taking action can be useful in helping you determine whether you are behaving in an ethical manner. These questions are:

- **If everyone took the same action, would society as a whole benefit?** You finish your bottle of energy drink and have to decide whether to toss the bottle out your car window or look for a trash receptacle. If everyone threw their trash wherever they felt like it, the world would soon look like a garbage dump. This would not benefit society.

- **Will your actions respect individuals or are you treating them as an ends to a means?** A casual acquaintance of yours (we'll call him Tom) works at the local arena in the ticket office. Your favorite band is coming to the arena, and tickets are already sold out. You don't really like Tom all that much, but you invite him over to your house for a barbeque and pretend to be his friend because you know he can get tickets that were held in reserve by management. Your treatment of the acquaintance is unethical because you are using him to satisfy your desire to see the concert.

- **Would an impartial observer consider your action fair to all parties involved in the decision?** Consider a scenario in which you go to a yard sale and find a rare t-shirt from an old rock concert that you know will sell for $4,000 on eBay. The person selling the shirt obviously is unaware of its value because it is priced at $4 and judging by the looks of his property, this person could use the money. You buy the shirt for $4 and leave. A neutral party analyzing this situation would probably not consider your actions ethical because the transaction was not fair to the person selling the t-shirt—you could have informed him of its value or offered him a more reasonable amount of money.

How does making ethical choices in a business setting differ from making personal ethical choices? Most personal ethical decisions involve few people, unless there is a great impact on society. When making ethical choices in the business world, careful consideration needs to be given to the stakeholders of the business. *Stakeholders* are those people or entities who are affected by the operations of a business. Before making an ethical choice for a business, you need to consider the effect it will have on all the stakeholders.

Imagine you are the plant manager of a small manufacturing company. The company has lost some key customers lately due to lower-priced competition from another company. You are under pressure to keep costs under control so that the company can compete effectively on price. You are concerned about the well-being of your employees if the plant has to make cutbacks due to lost sales. Your operation generates a small amount of liquid toxic waste, which costs $1,500 per month to have taken away. There is a storm drain out behind the plant into which you could empty the waste. Because it is summertime, there are thunderstorms almost every day. You think that if you dump the waste down the drain just before a thunderstorm, the water will flow through the storm drain and sufficiently dilute the waste, minimizing any hazard. It is illegal to dump this waste in your state, but you rate the likelihood of getting caught as extremely low. Eliminating the disposal costs would help you keep the price of your product competitive and potentially save jobs at your company. If your company is caught dumping wastes, the fines and the negative publicity may cause you to suspend business temporarily, make cutbacks in your production, or go out of business altogether. Although it is laudable to try and protect your friends' jobs, consider the potential effect on these stakeholders:

- **Customers**—Customers who depend on your product to run their businesses may have increased costs from seeking other suppliers or may not be able to operate at all if your company closes.

- **Suppliers**—Other companies who sell you raw materials are dependent upon your business. If your business were forced to close or cut back, their sales would be impacted and they might be forced to terminate employees or even cease operations.

- **Employees**—Getting caught might mean temporary or permanent lay-offs for your employees, and the negative publicity may keep your employees from getting other jobs if prospective employers think they were involved in the illegal activities.

- **Shareholders (investors)**—If the company loses money because of your actions, shareholders will not receive a fair return on their investments.

- **Financial lenders**—If the company suffers financial setbacks because of your actions, banks who have loaned your company money may not be repaid. This, in turn, can potentially affect the bank's stakeholders in a negative way.

- **Society**—Perhaps there is a leak in the storm drainage system and the toxic waste seeps into local wells used for drinking water before the runoff from the thunderstorms can dilute it. Or, the waste was not sufficiently diluted by the thunderstorms and ends up in local creeks killing off fish and wildlife.

Obviously, there are many factors to consider in a business ethics decision that might not immediately occur to you. No matter what ethical choices you make, some people are not going to agree with them. That doesn't necessarily mean you are right and they are wrong (and vice versa) because many ethical choices (unless prohibited by law) are a matter of personal interpretation. However, common sense dictates that you should always strive to obey the law (unless you look particularly fetching in an orange jumpsuit).

Objective 3
Decide Which Ethical Guidelines to Follow

With computers and the Internet becoming ubiquitous tools in our personal and work lives, more and more ethical decisions revolve around or involve technology. *Cyberethics* refers to an ethical code that is followed when using computers and the Internet. Just as with other ethical codes, cyberethics are subject to the influences and interpretations of personal ethics.

Why should I be concerned about cyberethics? Aside from being an "ethical" individual, you need to be aware of the ways that unethical people may try to take advantage of you in cyberspace. Unfortunately, the convenience and global communication provided by the Internet comes with a price—it is often easier for unethical people to operate using the Internet. Among the main reasons are:

- **Anonymity**—Communications and transactions on the Internet are often conducted without knowing who the parties are or who is involved—at least without certainty (see Figure 1.2). If you inquire about the status of an order at Amazon.com, you can feel somewhat secure that you are dealing with an official representative of Amazon.com. But what about someone you met in a chat room? All you might know about that person for certain is his screen name. So when he tells you that you can get a better deal at XYZBookDealers.com than on Amazon.com, how do you know you can trust that person?

- **Quick, convenient exchange of information**—When information is in digital form (such as music or a video), it is easy to reproduce it or transfer it from one person to another. This makes violating owner-ship rights much easier (and harder to detect because of the anonymity factor mentioned previously).

- **Impersonal nature of computer communications**—People often say things in an e-mail or on a blog that they wouldn't say to someone in person. For some individuals, impersonal communications are an excuse to communicate in an unprofessional or even hostile manner. This can lead to people making claims about others that are inaccu-rate or just blatantly untrue, which potentially increases the likeli-hood of legal action.

"On the Internet, nobody knows you're a dog."

Figure 1.2
Anonymity, while sometimes a good thing, can facilitate unethical behavior.

What cyberethics guidelines should I follow? Because of the potential for problems, most schools and businesses have adopted **acceptable use policies**—which are guidelines regarding usage of computer systems—relating to the use of their computing resources. Your school most likely has a policy similar to Figure 1.3 that you should be familiar with. You can usually find it on your school's Web site, either under the Information Technology department section or the Student Policies section. If you can't locate it, check with the help desk personnel at your school; they can likely direct you to the appropriate Web page.

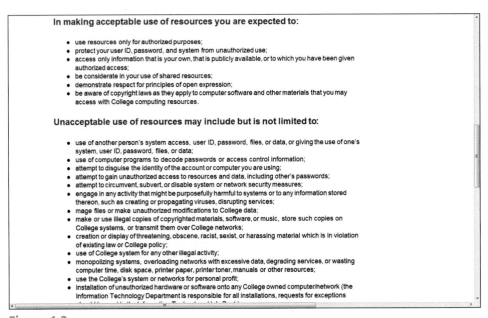

In making acceptable use of resources you are expected to:

- use resources only for authorized purposes;
- protect your user ID, password, and system from unauthorized use;
- access only information that is your own, that is publicly available, or to which you have been given authorized access;
- be considerate in your use of shared resources;
- demonstrate respect for principles of open expression;
- be aware of copyright laws as they apply to computer software and other materials that you may access with College computing resources.

Unacceptable use of resources may include but is not limited to:

- use of another person's system access, user ID, password, files, or data, or giving the use of one's system, user ID, password, files, or data;
- use of computer programs to decode passwords or access control information;
- attempt to disguise the identity of the account or computer you are using;
- attempt to gain unauthorized access to resources and data, including other's passwords;
- attempt to circumvent, subvert, or disable system or network security measures;
- engage in any activity that might be purposefully harmful to systems or to any information stored thereon, such as creating or propagating viruses, disrupting services;
- mage files or make unauthorized modifications to College data;
- make or use illegal copies of copyrighted materials, software, or music, store such copies on College systems, or transmit them over College networks;
- creation or display of threatening, obscene, racist, sexist, or harassing material which is in violation of existing law or College policy;
- use of College system for any other illegal activity;
- monopolizing systems, overloading networks with excessive data, degrading services, or wasting computer time, disk space, printer paper, printer toner, manuals or other resources;
- use the College's system or networks for personal profit;
- installation of unauthorized hardware or software onto any College owned computer/network (the Information Technology Department is responsible for all installations, requests for exceptions

Figure 1.3
An excerpt of the Acceptable Use of Technology Policy from Montgomery County Community College, Blue Bell, PA.

Among other things, these policies usually cover the following:

- Keeping your account access (logon ID and password) secure from others

- Not running a business with college assets

- Prohibition of attempts to gain access to portions of the computer systems you are not authorized to use

- Illegally copying legally protected materials, such as CDs and DVDs

- Creation, distribution, or display of threatening, obscene, racist, sexist, or harassing material

- Prohibiting the installation of unauthorized software on the college's computers

- Conducting any illegal activities with college computing systems

If you have a job, you should also familiarize yourself with your employer's policy because it may differ substantially from your school's policy. For instance, most schools consider any work products—such as research papers, poems, musical compositions, and so forth—generated with school computing resources to be the property of the students who created them, unless the students were paid to create the works. With many employers, any work products created using company-provided computing resources are deemed to be the property of the company, not the employees who created them. Certain colleges and universities consider faculty-generated work products to be the property of the institution.

What guidelines should I follow if my school or employer doesn't have an acceptable use policy? The Computer Ethics Institute—*www.computerethicsinstitute.org/*—which was founded by the Brookings Institute, developed a well-known set of guidelines you can follow. They are known as the Ten Commandments of Computer Ethics and they are listed in the table in Figure 1.4.

Thou shalt not use a computer to harm other people.
Thou shalt not interfere with other people's computer work.
Thou shalt not snoop around in other people's computer files.
Thou shalt not use a computer to steal.
Thou shalt not use a computer to bear false witness.
Thou shalt not copy or use proprietary software for which you have not paid.
Thou shalt not use other people's computer resources without authorization or proper compensation.
Thou shalt not appropriate other people's intellectual output.
Thou shalt think about the social consequences of the program you are writing or the system you are designing.
Thou shalt always use a computer in ways that ensure consideration and respect for your fellow humans.

Figure 1.4
The Ten Commandments of Computer Ethics.

In the absence of clear policies, following the Ten Commandments of Computer Ethics should help you steer clear of most unethical behavior. But the Ten Commandments won't necessarily cover every area of cyberethics, nor do they provide specific guidelines. For additional guidance, you should investigate the behavior guidelines known collectively as netiquette.

What is Netiquette? As usage of the Internet grew, users developed certain conventions for communicating and exchanging information over various Internet services, such as e-mail, online chats, online role-playing games, and so on. This collection of guidelines is known as *netiquette*. The core rules of netiquette are outlined at *www.albion.com/netiquette/* and like the Ten Commandments of Computer Ethics, are designed to show respect for other computer users and to avoid annoying or harassing other people in cyberspace. You should explore these rules on your own. A summary of the core rules are:

- **Remember the human**—It is easy to forget when you are staring at a computer screen that you are communicating with other human beings. Therefore, you should remember to treat others with respect;

when communicating, act as if the person on the other end is standing in front of you.

- **Adhere to the same standards of behavior online that you follow in real life**—Most people are law-abiding in real life. Emulate real life with your online actions.

- **Know where you are in cyberspace**—Rules vary according to what part of cyberspace you inhabit. Passing on unsubstantiated rumors about an upcoming Indiana Jones film is acceptable in a movie fan blog. Posting these rumors in a response to a journalist blog entry on the *New York Times* Web site is not. Be sure to learn the acceptable behaviors for the part of the Internet you are surfing.

- **Respect other people's time and bandwidth**—Forwarding piles of useless e-mail to friends and family wastes their time. Consider if something is important before you pass it on.

- **Make yourself look good online**—For a job interview, a first impression is important. That is why you always show up on time in appropriate attire and well groomed. On the Internet, often the only impression you make is through your writing. Be clear, concise, and on topic, and people will be more likely to respect you.

- **Share expert knowledge**—The Internet is mostly about sharing information. If you are an expert in an area, share your knowledge to help others. A great place to do this is Yahoo! Answers. In Figure 1.5, you can view an example of a question on Yahoo! Answers. Everyone is an expert at something!

Figure 1.5
Yahoo! Answers is a free service that allows people to post questions that other "experts" can answer. It is an excellent place to share your knowledge.

- **Help keep flame wars under control**—*Flaming* is when people express an opinion with strong emotion, usually when they disagree with someone else's opinion. *Flame wars* occur when two or more people keep escalating an argument by exchanging messages. It is best not to perpetuate arguments by keeping the communication going with escalating anger.

- **Respect other people's privacy**—Don't go snooping around other people's computer files without their permission.

- **Don't abuse your power**—If you have an advantage over others, such as access to all company e-mail, don't abuse the privilege by reading private e-mails.

- **Be forgiving of other people's mistakes**—If someone makes an error, point it out politely and constructively.

Being familiar with the proper rules of netiquette should ensure that you don't inadvertently disrupt the Internet experience of other people and should assist you in behaving in an ethical manner.

You will explore some of the biggest ethical challenges facing users of cyberspace, and you alone will decide how to behave in ethical situations. Neither anyone nor anything, including the content in this text, can tell you how to behave. However, if you are aware of the unethical behavior that can take place in cyberspace, you can protect yourself from unethical practices and be better able to make informed, personal ethical choices. Next, we explore one of the biggest areas of ethical concern in cyberspace—the misuse and theft of intellectual property.

Objective 4
Define Intellectual Property and Copyright

The Internet has a wealth of information. With a few clicks of the mouse, you can locate a picture of almost anything by using Google image search or by searching on photo sites such as Flickr. If you have to prepare a research paper on global warming, you can easily find millions of sources on the subject, including professionally written articles. Does that mean you can freely use all these wonderful resources you locate on the Internet? No, you can't, because they are most likely someone else's property. Just as you wouldn't walk over to your neighbor's house and steal his garden hose, you can't just take property you find on the Internet.

What is property? Property comes in two general types: real and personal. **Real property** is considered immovable, such as land or a home, and it is often called real estate. **Personal property** comes in two types: tangible and intangible. We are all familiar with **tangible personal property**, which is something that has substance—you can touch it— and can usually be moved from place to place. Examples of tangible personal property are this textbook, an iPod, or a car. If someone walks past your desk while you are in the bathroom at school and steals your iPod from your book bag, the action is easily recognizable as theft. However, what if someone tries to steal your ideas? This action moves into the realm of one of the biggest problems in cyberspace—the theft of intangible personal property or intellectual property.

What is intellectual property? *Intangible personal property* cannot be touched—or potentially even seen—yet, it still has value. Most intangible property is classified as intellectual property. *Intellectual property* is property that is a product of a person's mind and is usually considered an expression of human creativity. Examples of intellectual property are art, music, songs, movies (or any type of video), designs, logos, patents for inventions, formulas (or methods of production), and computer software. It is important to distinguish the intellectual property from the physical medium that carries it. A music CD is not intellectual property. The music that is contained on a CD is the intellectual property, whereas the CD itself is merely a transport or delivery device. Likewise, a poem is intellectual property, but the piece of paper on which it is written is not. Just as tangible personal property is protected by law from theft, intellectual property is also protected.

Who came up with the idea of protecting intellectual property?
John Locke was an English philosopher who developed many prominent theories about property rights, so perhaps he is considered the "father" of intellectual property rights. However, in the United States, the authors of the Constitution of the United States recognized that encouraging creativity was ultimately beneficial to society. As written in Article 1, Section 8 of the U.S. Constitution, Congress has the power to "promote the Progress of Science and useful Arts by securing for limited Times to Authors and Inventors the exclusive Right to their respective Writings and Discoveries." Giving a person exclusive control of the disposition of his intellectual property gives him a significant opportunity to make money from it. People might not be as motivated to generate creative ideas if they are unable to profit from them.

How is intellectual property categorized? Intellectual property is divided into broad categories: copyright, patents, trademarks and service marks, and trade dress. Each category has its own laws of protection.

According to Title 17 of the United States Code (17 USC 102), *copyright* protection can be granted to authors of "original works of authorship." In the United States and the European Union, copyrightable works include:

- Literary works, including computer software
- Musical works, including any accompanying words
- Dramatic works, including any accompanying music
- Pantomimes and choreographic works
- Pictorial, graphic, and sculptural works
- Motion pictures and other audiovisual works
- Sound recordings
- Architectural works

U.S. copyright law does not protect ideas, but rather the unique expression of an idea. You can't copyright common phrases, such as "bad boy" or "good girl," discoverable facts, such as water freezes at 32 degrees Fahrenheit, or old proverbs, such as, "To err is human, to forgive divine." However, you can copyright a creative twist on an old phrase, such as the one in Figure 1.6.

Figure 1.6
Although a parody of an old proverb, this phrase (offered on a t-shirt from Threadless.com) is sufficiently creative to allow it to be copyrighted.

Generic settings and themes of a story also can't be copyrighted. J.R.R. Tolkien wrote the *Lord of the Rings Trilogy*, which is about all types of monsters, wizards (Gandalf), and a young lad (Frodo) who overcomes great personal hardships and peril to save a land from the control of an evil being—Sauron. This didn't preclude writers, such as Terry Brooks, from creating stories like the *Sword of Shannara* in which a lad—Shea Ohmsford—overcomes personal peril and hardships to defeat an evil being—the Warlock Lord—who is bent on taking over the world. Mr. Brooks was merely precluded from using the same characters and plot lines as J.R.R. Tolkien but not the basic idea of a lone person overcoming odds against the forces of evil.

Patents are used to grant inventors the right to stop others from manufacturing, using, or selling (including importing) their inventions for a period of 20 years from the date the patent is filed. Generally, patents are not renewable but may be extended under certain circumstances. There are three basic types of patents:

- **Utility patents** are granted for inventing or discovering a novel and useful process, machine, product, or composition of matter (chemical entities and so on), which would include new improvements to existing products or methods.

- **Design patents** cover a new ornamental design for a product.

- **Plant patents** are granted for discovering or inventing a new type of plant.

A **_trademark_** is a word, phrase, symbol, or design—or a combination of all of these—that uniquely identifies and differentiates the goods of one party from those of another. A **_service mark_** is essentially the same as a trademark, but it applies to a service as opposed to a product. The Nike swoosh and McDonald's Golden Arches, shown in Figure 1.7, are both trademarks, whereas the FedEx logo is a service mark.

Similar to a trademark, a **_trade dress_** applies to the visual appearance of a product or its packaging. This would include interior decorations or the external design and ornamentation of a building, such as restaurants. The signature look of a TGI Fridays restaurant—red and white striped table cloths and the eclectic décor—or the unique shape of the Coca Cola glass bottle, shown in Figure 1.7, are examples of trade dress.

Figure 1.7
Instantly recognizable images such as the Nike swoosh, McDonald's Golden Arches, the Federal Express logo, and the Coca Cola glass bottle, all need protection from other companies that may try to produce look-alikes.

If I work for a company and develop intellectual property, do I own it? The answer to this question depends on the terms of your employment contract with your employer. Most companies—pharmaceutical companies, advertising agencies, movie production companies, and so on—in which intellectual property that has potential develops during employment, require their employees to sign agreements that any intellectual property developed while working for the company becomes the company's property. Mattel, the makers of Barbie dolls, filed a lawsuit against MGA Entertainment, which makes the successful line of Bratz dolls shown in Figure 1.8. Mattel alleged that Carter Bryant, the designer of the Bratz dolls, came up with the design for them while working at Mattel. Mr. Bryant's employment agreement with Mattel stipulated that Mattel was the owner of anything he designed while employed by Mattel. The court found for Mattel in this action and granted them damages of $90 million related to the violation of the employment agreement that Mr. Bryant had with Mattel. The court also awarded Mattel $10 million for copyright infringement. Mattel will now probably seek an injunction to stop MGA from making the Bratz dolls. Before you invent a new gasoline additive to solve the energy crisis, make sure you don't have an agreement in place with your employer that means it owns it instead of you!

Figure 1.8
Who actually owns the designs to the Bratz line of dolls depended on whether the creator designed them while he was working at Mattel.

How long does copyright last? Current copyright law in the United States grants copyright for the life of the author (creator) plus 70 years for original works. ***Works made for hire*** or ***works of corporate authorship***, which is when a company or person pays you to create a work and then that person or company owns the copyright to the work when it is completed, have copyright terms of 120 years after creation or 95 years after publication, whichever is shorter. After you die, the copyrights you own are transferred to your heirs. Therefore, if you write a best-selling novel in 2015 and die in 2082, your heirs can continue to earn money from the copyrighted novel until the year 2152. Copyright laws and terms of copyright are modified from time to time. The table in Figure 1.9 summarizes significant U.S. legislation on copyright.

Name of Law (Act)	Significant Points
Copyright Act of 1790	First U.S. copyright law—Copyright term of 14 years with 14-year renewal established.
Copyright Act of 1909	Extended copyright term to 28 years with a 28-year available renewal.
Copyright Act of 1976	Term extended to either 75 years or life of author plus 50 years. Renewal option eliminated. Registration no longer required.
Copyright Term Extension Act (CTEA) of 1998	Term now life of author plus 70 years. Works of corporate authorship now 120 years after creation or 95 years after publication, whichever endpoint is earlier. Extended term to 95 years from publication for works published prior to January 1, 1978.
Digital Millennium Copyright Act (DMCA) of 1998	Increased penalties for copyright violation on the Internet. Criminalized the production and dissemination of technology, devices, or services that could be used to circumvent measures that protect access or duplication of copyrighted works.
Artist's Rights and Theft Prevention Act of 2005	Designed to prohibit the piracy of movies by filming them in a theater. Made it illegal to distribute unreleased software—including beta software—which will later be sold for profit.

Figure 1.9
Major U.S. legislation affecting copyright.

If someone owns copyright to work, what exactly do they own?
Copyright holders own a bundle of rights that grant them the ability to exclusively do things with the copyrighted work. Section 106 of the U.S. 1976 Copyright Act grants these specific rights to a copyright holder:

- **Reproducing the work**—This means copying the entire work or just part of the work. Violations of this right may involve burning a copy of a music CD, photocopying a magazine article, copying software DVDs, or printing a cartoon character, such as Calvin from the *Calvin and Hobbes* cartoon strip, on a messenger bag using a Web site such as *www.cafepress.com.*

- **Preparing derivative works based upon the original work**—This means developing any media based on the original work regardless of what form the original is in. The X-Men were originally characters in a comic book, but they now appear in movies and video games. Andrew Lloyd Webber's *Phantom of the Opera* was developed into a movie script from the original play. You can't develop a derivative work without the copyright holder's permission, so you cannot just develop and sell your own movie script based on the X-Men or *Phantom of the Opera.*

- **Distributing the work to the public**—This means any method of distribution but usually involves selling the work. However, the copyright holder could also loan, rent, or give away the work. Copying a music CD and selling it (or even giving it) to your friend would be a violation of this right.

- **Public performance of the work**—Obviously, this applies to any audiovisual work such as plays, movies, songs, choreographic works, and literary readings. In the case of audio recordings, this also means digital audio transmission. You can't put a copy of the latest Batman movie up on YouTube or show the movie at your annual company meeting without permission of the copyright holder because that would constitute a public performance.

- **Public display of the work**—This usually applies to works of art such as paintings, photographs, and sculpture. Putting copies of photographs that someone else holds copyright to on your blog is a violation of this right.

When does copyright protection begin? Copyright begins when a work is created and fixed into a tangible, physical form, as illustrated in Figure 1.10. For example, if you make a video of your cat, as soon as you save the video to tape, your hard drive, or a DVD, the video is subject to copyright protection. There is no need for the video to be registered or even published for it to be protected.

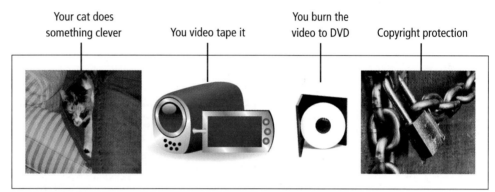

Your cat does something clever   You video tape it   You burn the video to DVD   Copyright protection

Figure 1.10
The copyright formula in action.

Can rights to a copyrighted work be sold? Rights to copyrighted work obviously have value if there is a demand for the work. Rights can be sold or granted for free to various individuals or entities in perpetuity or for a limited period of time. For instance, if you make a video of your band and your band is going to appear at a local bar, you might grant the bar owner the right to play your video in his bar for a specific period of time leading up to your performance. Or, you might grant the right to produce and sell DVDs of your performance to a distributor such as CD Baby—*www.cdbaby.com*—so you can earn some money from your fans. When your band appears at a local Battle of the Bands competition, you might grant the promoter the right to sell your CDs to fans at the concert and provide you with a percentage of the profits. Figure 1.11 shows many of the ways you can sell or grant rights to your copyrighted work.

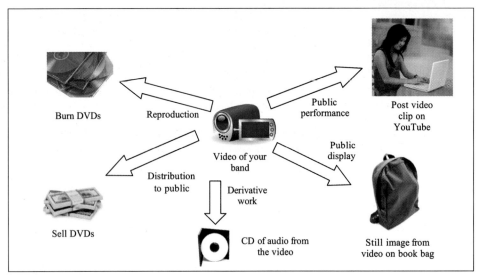

Figure 1.11
Exercising some of your rights from your copyrighted video.

Is buying a copyrighted work, such as a music CD or a book, the same as buying the copyright? In most cases you will encounter, buying a copyrighted work does not mean you are buying the copyright. When you buy a copyrighted item, such as a book, you own only the physical item. The copyright is unaffected and still resides with the copyright holder. Pearson Education, Inc. owns the copyright to this book. However, buying copyrighted works is covered by a rule of law known as the ***first sale doctrine***. You have the right to sell, lend, give away, or otherwise dispose of the item you purchase. This is the legal principle that allows public libraries to operate by lending out copyrighted material.

When you buy software, all you have usually bought is a license to install the software and use it on a specific number of computers. There may be other restrictions such as prohibition against using the software for profit. Check your license. For music CDs, all you have bought is the right to listen to the music in a private setting—your home, car, and so on. You cannot broadcast the music publicly, such as on the Internet. When you buy a DVD of a movie, again you have just bought the right to view the movie privately. You don't have the right to set up a screening for 50 of your closest friends in a local bar.

Are all works, such as music, books, movies, and so on, protected by copyright? Some works that were created never had a copyright holder. Examples are old traditional folk songs, the origin of which is unknown. For copyrighted works, they can lose their copyright protection. The term of protection can expire, the owner might not renew the copyright to extend the term—if renewal was available—or the owner may have intentionally relinquished the rights. Works without copyright protection are considered in the ***public domain***. Works in the public domain are considered public property and therefore, anyone can modify, distribute, copy them, and even sell them for profit.

When is a work considered in the public domain? It is difficult sometimes to determine when works enter the public domain. Factors that can influence the determination are the date of publication, whether the work was published, if copyright was applied for, if a notice is published, and many other factors. Copyright terms vary between countries, but many countries have similar laws. Under U.S. and European Union laws, a work is probably in the public domain if the following is true:

- The work was created or published before January 1, 1923 or at least 95 years before January 1 of the current year, whichever is later.

- The last surviving author died at least 70 years before January 1 of the current year.

However, there are exceptions to these rules. Therefore, you should probably only consider a work in the public domain that has provable, objective evidence that it is in the public domain or is clearly stated as being in the public domain.

The basic assumption you need to make is that all intellectual property you find on the Internet is protected by copyright (unless otherwise stated).

Objective 5
Understand Permissible Use of Copyrighted Material

Under what circumstances can copyrighted material be used? Many Web sites that contain copyrighted material also contain lengthy legal documents that delineate the *terms of use*—the terms governing your use of material—for the material that you download from the site. It is important for you to find and read the terms of use *before* using any copyrighted material on the site. Failure to read the terms of use does not absolve you from liability for using copyrighted material without permission. The terms of use Web page from Photos.com, as shown in Figure 1.12, clearly spells out your rights regarding photos downloaded from its Web site.

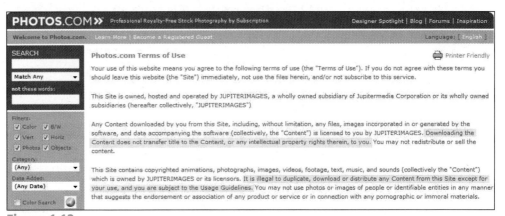

Figure 1.12
Excerpt of the Terms of Use from Photos.com. Notice how the highlighted portions severely limit your actions.

What if a Web site does not have terms of use? Ferreting out the terms of use on a particular site can sometimes be tricky. Look for links that say, Terms of Use, Restrictions, Copyright, Rules, FAQ, or even Contact Us. Sometimes, the usage terms are not displayed until you attempt to download copyrighted material. If you have done a thorough search and can't find them, then follow the instructions for contacting the organization that maintains the Web site and ask about the terms of use.

Can you use copyrighted material if it isn't permitted in the terms of use or there are no terms of use? Copyright holders can always grant permission to use copyrighted material to an individual or organization. Depending upon the material used and the specific nature of the usage, there may be a payment necessary to secure the rights to the copyrighted work. Sometimes though, simply asking permission is enough to get you the rights to use the work for a specific purpose free of charge.

Whom do you contact for permission? Whom to contact to obtain permission depends on the nature of the intellectual property. Sometimes it can be difficult to tell who actually owns the copyright, or the particular rights you need, to a piece of media. The creator may not be the copyright holder any longer. They may have sold their rights to another party.

The table in Figure 1.13 provides some suggestions about possible contacts for permission.

	Type of Media	Who to Contact
	Books or periodicals	Publisher or author
	Web site text	Webmaster, Web site owner, or author
	Photos, sculpture, paintings, or other art	Artist or photographer, publisher if it's print media, museum or gallery management if it's on display, or Web site owner
	Movies or video	Uploader if it's original video on a Web site, the production company (may not own the rights, but should know who does), film distributor, or screenwriter

Figure 1.13
Contacts for various types of media.

What information is provided in a permission request? The most important items to include are a description of the work you are requesting permission to use—the exact parts if the entire work is not being requested—and the scope of your use. Be sure to include all of these key points:

- **Who you are**—Are you an individual or requesting permission on behalf of an organization or business? Be sure to include complete contact information (name, address, phone number, and e-mail address).

- **Which work you are requesting permission to use**—Make sure to describe the work completely and accurately. "That cool picture you posted on Flickr" isn't going to be sufficient because the photographer might have hundreds of pictures posted online!

- **Complete details of your usage of the work**—The copyright holder will be interested in why you are using the work, the context in which the work will be used, if the work is being used as part of a money-making project, where the work will be used (Web site, book, magazine, and so on), how frequently the work will be used, and if you are making any modifications to the work. You may be required to illustrate exactly how the work will be used, such as showing a mock-up of a Web page or the layout of a page in a book.

- **The timing of the request**—Be sure to indicate the date you intend to begin using the work and suggest a deadline for responding to the request. This might help speed up a response to your request for permission.

Be sure you receive a written response to your request authorizing the usage you requested. You should never assume that no response is an indication of a tacit approval on the part of the copyright holder. Remember, copyright holders are under no obligation to grant your request or even to respond to it. As the owner of the work, they alone decide if and when it can be used by someone else. Therefore, you should always have a back-up plan in case your request for permission is denied or ignored.

Objective 6
Describe Copyright Infringement

What happens if you use copyrighted material without permission of the copyright holder? A violation of the holder's rights is known as *copyright infringement*. According to section 501 of Title 17 of the United States Code (17 USC 501), "Anyone who violates any of the exclusive rights of the copyright owner . . . is an infringer of the copyright or right of the author." Examples of copyright infringement are:

- Right-clicking on a photo you find on a Web site and saving it to your hard drive,

- Copying a music CD and giving it to a friend,

- Using a peer-to-peer file sharing service, such as BitTorrent, to download a new action movie—in other words, you did not buy the movie from an authorized agent of the copyright holder.

- Taking a photograph of a work displayed in a museum and using it in a work you are publishing.

- Setting up a fan Web site dedicated to your favorite TV show that features clips from the TV show and the theme music from the show.

- Copying a copyrighted software program and giving it to your friend.

- Singing a copyrighted song in a video with your friends and then posting it on YouTube.

When judges consider cases of infringement, they generally examine the extent to which there is a substantial similarity between the copyrighted work and the infringing work. Obviously, if you copy an image from the Internet or burn a copy of a CD, that would be an exact copy and clearly is infringement. What if you wrote a play based on characters from *Star Wars*? Or, what if you wrote a story with a similar plot to an episode of your favorite TV show? The courts will have to determine how similar the characters and plot are to the copyrighted works and if infringement exists. This is a subjective process, and infringement cases are usually decided on the merits of each case.

Is putting a URL that points to a copyrighted Web site on a site (such as a MySpace page) considered copyright infringement? A URL is a specific direction for finding a specific Web page on the Internet. It is not debatable or open to interpretation, and therefore, it is considered a fact. Because facts cannot be copyrighted, you can list all the textual URLs you want on your Web site without committing copyright infringement. However, be sure you do not take copyrighted material, such as a logo or character, to use as a picture link to a Web site, such as using a picture of Mickey Mouse to link to the Disney Web site, as this may constitute infringement.

What are the most common types of copyright infringement in cyberspace? Illegally copying or using software, music, video, and photographs top the list of digital rights violations on the Internet. Aside from the copyright laws mentioned earlier, many court cases have helped frame the context of digital copyright infringement in the United States. The table in Figure 1.14 lists some of these cases.

Year	Case Name	Major Issue(s)	Significant Outcomes
1976	*Sony v. Universal Studios*	Universal alleged that manufacturing and marketing of VCRs allowed people to violate their copyrights on television shows and movies.	Time shifting (watching a show at a different time than when it was broadcast) did not have a significant effect on the market for the copyrighted work. Time shifting for personal use is permissible.
1999	*RIAA v. Diamond Multimedia Systems Inc.*	Recording Industry Association of America (RIAA) alleged that the Rio portable music player (MP3 player) allowed users to violate music copyright.	Copying a recording to make it portable is deemed "space shifting" and permissible under U.S. copyright law.
2001	*RIAA v. Napster*	RIAA sued Napster for allowing users to violate copyright by downloading copyrighted songs.	Napster was forced to shut down because they were unable to block 100% of illegal downloads of copyrighted material. Napster later reopened as a site that sells legally licensed music.
2005	*MGM Studios, Inc. v. Grokster, Ltd.*	MGM and a group of other movie studios, songwriters, recording companies, and music publishers sued Grokster and Streamcast for allowing members to download copyrighted music and videos.	The U.S. Supreme court decided that peer-to-peer file sharing companies Grokster and Streamcast can be sued for copyright infringement when their users illegally exchange copyrighted files.

Figure 1.14
Major court cases involving digital rights violations.

How are music and video copyrights usually infringed? The major sources of infringement for music and video are:

- **Peer-to-peer file sharing**—Peer-to-peer (P2P) networks, such as Limewire, BitTorrent, and Morpheus, are virtual networks deployed across the Internet that enable two computers running common P2P software to connect directly with each other and access files stored on the other computer's hard drive. These networks provide users with access to files on millions of other computers and have the ability to upload and download files from multiple computers simultaneously. Although peer-to-peer networks can be used to exchange files legally, they are often used to exchange copyrighted materials such as music and movies.

- **Direct exchange or copying**—Many people freely burn copies of CDs and DVDs for their friends or allow their friends to copy the entire contents of their portable media player (iPod).

- **Uploading to file-sharing sites**—Many of the files on sharing sites such as YouTube are from copyrighted material. Just because you can record a television show for personal use because of the *Sony v. Universal Studios* decision, it doesn't mean you can upload it on YouTube for everyone to watch.

Are people who upload music videos or clips from TV shows to YouTube liable for copyright infringement? Although many people think that YouTube would be responsible for any infringement, anyone who uploads copyrighted material could be held responsible. Currently, Viacom has lodged a $1 billion damage suit against YouTube and its parent company Google for copyright infringement related to the many television shows and movies to which it holds copyright. The suit alleges that YouTube has permitted 160,000 clips of unauthorized Viacom-owned content to be viewed billions of times. Google is defending itself by pointing to the 1998 Digital Millennium Copyright Act, which is designed to protect Internet companies from copyrighted content uploaded by their users. If YouTube wins the suit, Viacom could still go after individual uploaders or even viewers of the material for compensation. And if YouTube loses the suit, it may have to come to the uploaders for compensation.

Why would YouTube be able to collect damages from users for uploading protected content? Although users might not have paid attention when uploading videos, they did agree not to infringe copyright when uploading the files, as shown in see Figure 1.15. Therefore, YouTube has potential legal recourse to recover damages from users who ignore the terms of use on their Web site. If you have uploaded copyrighted material to YouTube or any other file sharing site, you should remove it immediately.

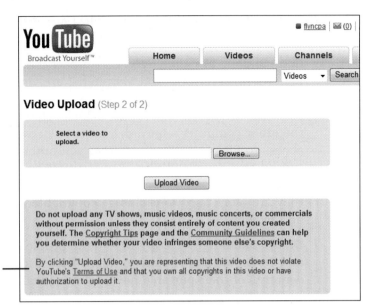

You said you have copyright to the video or permission to upload it. Do you?

Figure 1.15
Those who upload videos to YouTube agree not to infringe copyright.

Why would a band object to uploading a music video to YouTube or a Web site? Wouldn't it be free publicity for them? Each time someone plays a video that is uploaded to a Web site, the performer (singer or band), the songwriter, and the music publisher lose money. If the person listening to the song forgoes buying the music, the performer and his record company lose money. However, a song played on a Web site is considered a live performance. Songwriters and music publishers (organizations that promote songwriters' compositions to record companies and take a cut of royalty payments) are entitled to a royalty every time a song is played live, on the radio (or other broadcast medium), or on the Internet. Normally, royalty fees are paid by radio stations and other entities performing music to Performing Rights Organizations (PROs) such as The American Society of Composers, Authors and Publishers (ASCAP), Broadcast Music, Inc. (BMI), and SoundExchange. The PROs then forward the royalties to the songwriters and music publishers. Because you are not paying royalties to a PRO when the video is viewed on YouTube, someone is losing revenue.

How significant is the loss of revenue from music and video infringement? It is difficult to quantify the impact on revenue. A recent June, 2008 study by the University of Hertfordshire revealed that on average there are 842 illegally copied songs on the average 14-to-24-year-olds' digital music players. This accounts for 48 percent of the average collection of music. So potentially, music revenue might be cut in *half* by illegal file swapping. If you copy 40 songs from a friend's iPod instead of buying them on iTunes for $.99 each, you've potentially deprived numerous entities (record companies, performers, and songwriters) of $39.60 of revenue.

How are the rights of software copyright holders usually violated?
Illegally using copyrighted software is often referred to as *software piracy*.
If you have ever given a friend a copy of a copyrighted software program
to install on his computer, then you are intimately familiar with a common
method of infringement. The Business Software Alliance (*www.bsa.org*),
an organization that has among its goals the prevention of software
piracy, provides a few other examples of software piracy that you may
not have thought about:

- Taking advantage of upgrade offers without possessing a required older version of the software

- Using software designed specifically for academic or non-commercial use for commercial purposes

- Installing a licensed copy of software on more computers than the license permits

- Downloading copyrighted software from peer-to-peer networks

- Buying pirated copies of software on Internet auction sites

- Counterfeiting software (copying it for the express purpose of selling it as if it were the real, licensed product)

- Selling computers preloaded with illegal copies of software already installed

You need to exercise caution when buying software online to ensure that
it is a real, fully licensed copy. Otherwise you might not even be able to
use the software that you bought. Most modern software requires a serial number for installation. And usually, the first time you launch the
software after installation, this serial number is checked against a database to ensure the software has not been installed on more computers
than the license allows. This is a form of *digital rights management*.
If you are buying illegally copied software on the Internet, you might not
be able to activate it because too many other people have already
installed it with the serial number you have.

How widespread is software piracy? In some countries, such as China,
it can be described as rampant. As the table in Figure 1.16 shows, piracy rates can exceed 90 percent in some areas of the world. Although less
of a problem in the United States on a percentage basis, the U.S. still
leads the world in lost revenue from software piracy.

Country	Percentage of Installed Software that Is Pirated	Estimated Economic Loss (U.S. $ in Millions)
Bangladesh	92	$92
Brazil	59	$1,617
China	82	$6,664
France	42	$2,601
Kenya	81	$28
India	69	$2,025
Russia	73	$4,123
United Kingdom	26	$1,837
United States	20	$8,040

Figure 1.16
2007 software piracy statistics for selected countries per the Business Software Alliance.

Why is photographic infringement widespread on the Internet? The Web is a visual medium. Therefore, many pictures are displayed on Web sites. With the proliferation of camera phones and according to IDC, a marketing intelligence firm, forecasted sales of 8.5 million digital cameras per year by 2011, it is not surprising that millions of photos are uploaded to the Internet every day. Photo-sharing sites like Flickr, Picasa, and Photobucket give anyone the ability to post and share photos online. Of course the widespread availability of images also gives rise to people appropriating them for their own use. Need a picture of the Grand Canyon for your PowerPoint presentation? Using Google image search or Flickr's search feature will probably enable you to find an appropriate image. And right-clicking and saving it to your hard drive is simple, which is a major reason why infringement of photo copyright is so widespread on the Internet.

Who owns the copyright to a photo? When the photo is taken, the photographer owns the copyright, assuming the photographer was taking photographs in a public place or had permission from the property owner to take photos. In the U.S., you are free to take photos in public places such as streets, public parks, or sidewalks. Property owners can prohibit photography on their premises, so be sure to enquire about the right to take photographs in privately owned space. But if the photographer was working on a "work for hire" basis (his employer was paying him to take the photos), usually the copyright will belong to the employer.

Do people in the photograph have any rights to the photograph? The Fourth Amendment to the U.S. Constitution and various other laws and court cases have recognized Americans' rights to certain amounts of privacy. Being photographed without your consent generally falls under the realm of privacy. Usually, if a photographer takes a picture with you in it that he knows he wants to sell for publication, he will ask you to sign a ***model release***. A model release usually grants the photographer the right to use an image of the model (or subject of the photo) commercially. If a picture of you is published without your consent, you might have the basis for a lawsuit. However, be aware that there are many times when you agree to allow your photograph to be taken and used commercially (usually for publicity). You may agree to these conditions when you enter a contest, buy a ticket for a museum, or enter an event such as a marathon or a concert. So make sure you read the conditions of sign-up forms and the back of tickets to ensure you understand any rights you are surrendering.

What happens when a photographer sells or transfers rights to a photograph? Often the photographer will sell the rights to the image for publication on a Web site, in a magazine, and so on. Selling the rights might not transfer copyright depending upon the type of rights sold. The most common rights are:

- **Exclusive photo rights**—The purchaser of these rights is the only one who may use the photo. These rights can be limited to a specific industry or might specify no publication in vehicles of competing organizations. For instance, you may take a photo of Old Faithful that a travel magazine wishes to use on their cover. The rights may preclude you from selling exclusive rights to other travel periodicals but not from selling the rights to a souvenir company.

- **One time or lease rights**—Rights to photos can be sold for a certain number of instances (someone can publish the photo three times in their magazine) or for a specific duration (display the photo for a year on their Web site).

- **All rights**—This transfers all rights to the photo to the buyer.

How do you know if a photo on the Web is copyrighted? Usually information is attached to a photo to indicate it is copyrighted or that all rights are reserved. If there is not information attached, the safest course of action is to assume that the photo is protected by copyright. Figure 1.17 shows an example of information attached to a photo that is copyright protected. Or, there may be information that says the photo is in the public domain or free for anyone to use. If there is no information on copyright, your safest assumption is that you can't use it without permission of the copyright holder.

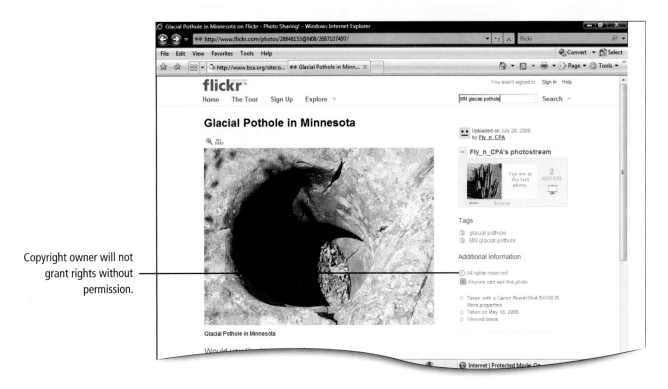

Copyright owner will not grant rights without permission.

Figure 1.17
Although this photographer's work is available to anyone searching Flickr, he has reserved all rights so you cannot use his photo without permission.

Objective 7
Explain the Consequences of Copyright Infringement and How to Avoid Infringement

What happens to people who infringe on someone's copyright?
Infringing copyright risks a potentially long and costly legal battle. At best, you might receive a slap on the wrist, but the worst-case scenarios can involve large fines and jail time. The penalties vary depending upon the laws relating to the type of property being infringed and the country whose laws are in effect. In the United States (17 USC 504), statutory civil penalties for software infringement can be up to $150,000 per software program copied. And this is in addition to the $250,000 fine and 5-year jail sentence for the criminal charges that can be levied against you by the United States government.

How will you know if someone thinks you have infringed on their copyright? If you used a picture of Mickey Mouse on your Web site without permission, you might receive a *cease and desist letter* from the Walt Disney Corporation. This letter is a request to immediately stop the alleged infringement. The letter should describe the alleged infringement and require you to reply by a certain date to indicate that the infringement has ceased. If you receive such a letter, you should take it seriously. In our example, be sure you remove the picture of Mickey from your Web site and respond by the due date in a letter indicating what you have done to stop the infringement.

What if you don't believe you committed copyright infringement?
Seek competent legal advice from an attorney specializing in intellectual
property law and have the attorney assist you in crafting a reply to the
cease and desist letter explaining your side of the story. You may be able
to prove you did not infringe if you have proof you received permission
to use the material or if you can make a successful argument for a fair
use exception (we discuss fair use later in this chapter). Because the
next step taken against you might be a formal legal action, the help of
an attorney is critical at this stage. If the issuer of the cease and desist
letter is not satisfied with your response or your actions, the next step is
most likely a lawsuit against you.

**What happens if a person loses a court case and is found guilty of
infringement?** If someone is found guilty of infringement, the court
might provide for the following types of relief for the copyright holder:

- Issue an *injunction*—a court order prohibiting a certain action—that
  forces you to stop the infringement. This can include recalling or
  destroying all copies of printed matter containing the infringing material, stopping the performance or display of the infringing work (in the
  case of music, a play, art, or a video), removing the material from
  your Web site, and so on.

- Confiscation and destruction of the infringing items, such as an entire
  piece of artwork, t-shirts you were selling with infringing images, and
  so on.

- Make the violator pay actual damages or statutory damages per the
  copyright statues. *Actual damages* are provable losses sustained by
  the company such as lost revenue. *Statutory damages* are pre-
  scribed by law and in the U.S. currently range from $750 to $30,000.
  However, if the court finds there was *willful infringement* (such as
  intentionally ignoring a copyright notice that was clearly evident),
  under U.S. law, the penalties can be increased up to $150,000.

Why would anyone risk copyright infringement? With such serious
penalties, you would think everyone would respect copyright. Why run
the risk of a large fine just to enhance a MySpace page with a cool
image? Here are a few reasons why students have indicated that they
risk copyright infringement:

- **Low likelihood of getting caught**—People often base their actions on
  their chances of being discovered. If you download three songs from a
  P2P Web site or copy a CD from a friend, are you likely to get caught?
  Probably not, but that still doesn't make it an ethical action. You are
  still depriving an artist of his livelihood. However, some people will
  always commit acts that are illegal (or generally accepted as unethical) if they think they can escape notice.

- **Everyone is doing it (the tax cheat defense)**—Many U.S. citizens
  who cheat on their taxes state the reason for doing so as "Everyone
  else does it so why should I miss out?" However, numerous surveys
  have been done that prove that the vast majority of Americans do not
  cheat on their taxes. But, this herd mentality tends to affect some
  people's actions, especially if the likelihood of getting caught is low.

- **No one would come after an individual**—Many students are under the impression that only large corporations with a lot of money are being sued for copyright infringement. But if you ask the over 20,000 individuals who have been sued for illegal file sharing by the RIAA since 2003, you might have a different opinion. Most of these cases were settled out of court for amounts ranging from $3,000 to $4,000, but court awards have gone higher. The RIAA is tending to target **supernodes** (people who offer thousands of music files on P2P networks for sharing) for their legal action, but they can just as easily target you for downloading a couple of CDs of songs.

- **I'm only downloading one song . . . it isn't worth that much**— Whether you are stealing one candy bar from a convenience store or a Corvette from the mall is irrelevant. They are both still crimes. Because copyright infringement is also prohibited by law, copying one song is still stealing.

Now let's explore the concept of fair use, which is one way (besides obtaining permission to use copyrighted material) that you can steer clear of copyright infringement and keep yourself from being tied up in unnecessary legal entanglements.

Objective 8
Define Fair Use

Are there any instances in which you can use copyrighted work without permission of the copyright holder? In original copyright law, there were no exceptions to obtaining the copyright holder's permission to use the work. However, a number of court cases over the years served to develop the doctrine of fair use. In 1976, the concept of fair use was added to the copyright laws and is now codified in section 107 of the Copyright Act (17 USC 107). **Fair use** provides for people to use portions of a copyrighted work for specific purposes without receiving prior permission from the copyright holder. However, there are no specific rules on exactly what amount of use constitutes fair use, which means each case has to be decided on its own merits.

What types of activities constitute fair use? A list of examples of approved fair use activities from U.S. court cases is provided in the 1961 Report of the Register of Copyrights on the General Revision of the U.S. Copyright Law. Although this list is not all-encompassing, it provides a good start for evaluating fair use activities. Following are some examples:

- Quotation of excerpts in a review or criticism for purposes of illustration or comment.

- Quotation of short passages in a scholarly or technical work, for illustration or clarification of the author's observations.

- Use in a parody of some of the content of the work parodied.

- Summary of an address or article, with brief quotations, in a news report.

- Reproduction by a library of a portion of a work to replace part of a damaged copy.

- Reproduction by a teacher or student of a small part of a work to illustrate a lesson; this is commonly known as educational fair use.

- Reproduction of a work in legislative or judicial proceedings or reports.

- Incidental and fortuitous reproduction in a newsreel or broadcast, of a work located in the scene of an event being reported.

Copying a CD or DVD that you own to serve only as a backup copy in case yours is damaged is also usually—but not definitively—considered fair use, as established by certain court cases. However, under the Digital Millennium Copyright Act, it is illegal to circumvent any technology that is employed to prevent media from being copied. Therefore, if you have a CD, DVD, or MP3 file that has copy protection technology—also known as digital rights management—in place, you are not legally entitled to copy it even though there are probably software programs available on the Web that could allow you to do so. This represents a conflict between the body of case law and a legal statute and remains a source of confusion and frustration for consumers.

What factors do the courts consider when determining fair use?
There are four factors used to consider whether usage of copyrighted material is considered fair use:

- **The purpose and character of the use**—A major factor here is whether the user will profit from the work. Profiting from the work usually precludes a fair use exemption except in the case of transformative works (like parody). For use to be **transformative**, the work must be altered in some manner that causes the user or viewer of the work to derive another meaning from the work. Satire is a technique that is used to poke fun at political views, moral principles, or social mores usually in an attempt to provoke change or draw attention to a particular issue. Parody is considered transformative and therefore is usually viewed as fair use.

- **The nature of the copyrighted work**—Factual works have less copyright protection under the fair use doctrine than creative or fictional works. Commonly known or discoverable facts cannot be copyrighted although a unique expression of facts can be copyrighted. "The sky is blue" or "The diameter of the moon is 2,160 miles" can't be copyrighted. Therefore, excerpts from factual works are much more likely to be considered fair use.

- **The amount and substantiality of the portion used in relation to the copyrighted work as a whole**—The courts look primarily at whether you used only as little of the work as possible to accomplish your goal. You should also stay away from using parts of a work that are key to making it special or creative. For instance, using a small passage from *Gone with the Wind* that is incidental to the main plot would most likely be considered fair use. Using key lines from the last scene where Rhett leaves Scarlett would be viewed much less favorably.

- **The effect of the use upon the potential market for or value of the copyrighted work**—If your use would affect the ability of the copyright holder to sell or otherwise profit from his protected work, this tends to argue against fair use because there is little that is "fair" about affecting someone's ability to earn money. Copying a song from a band's CD and posting it on YouTube as a video (with still pictures of the band) would not be considered fair use. Although you could argue that using a different medium for the work (video) is transformative because people can listen to the song for free on YouTube, you damage the market value of the song.

Does being a student who uses educational (academic) fair use give me a defense for using any copyrighted material I want? Unfortunately, this is what many students and some instructors think. However, even educational fair use has to be reasonable and meet the four tests cited previously to be deemed a defense against copyright infringement.

Educational fair use greatly facilitates teaching and learning, which tends to be a fluid process. As lesson plans change frequently based on current events, teachers and students might find it difficult to obtain the permissions they need in a timely fashion to ensure content in classroom discussions, multimedia, and research papers are current. Because there are no fixed guidelines on the quantity of material that can be used and still be considered fair use, various groups of educators have met to develop guidelines to assist teachers and students. The Consortium of College and University Media Centers developed suggested guidelines for various types of media, excerpts of which are summarized in the table in Figure 1.18. The full text of the guidelines can be found on the American Distance Education Consortium Web site at *www.adec.edu.*

Media	Quantity
Motion media	Up to 10% or 3 minutes, whichever is less
Text material	Up to 10% or 1,000 words, whichever is less
Music, lyrics, and music videos	Up to 10%, but in no event more than 30 seconds, of the music and lyrics from an individual musical work (or in the aggregate of extracts from an individual work)
Illustrations and photographs	a) One artist: No more than 5 images b) Collections of works: No more than 10% or 15 images, whichever is less
Numerical data sets (databases and spreadsheets)	Up to 10% or 2,500 fields or cell entries, whichever is less

Figure 1.18
Suggested fair use guidelines.

Again, these are only suggested guidelines and depending upon the individual case, you may be able to make a successful argument under the fair use doctrine to use a greater percentage of a given work. Many educational institutions publish their own guidelines, so be sure to inquire about your school's guidelines.

Objective 9
Explain How to Protect Your Work Against Infringement

What work do I have that could be infringed upon? The answer to this question depends on whether or not you are creating valuable intellectual property. Are you a prolific, capable photographer who uploads thousands of images to Flickr? Are you writing a blog that is read by a lot of people every day? Are you posting original research that you have done to Web pages on the Internet? Do you have a band and have you posted videos of original performances on YouTube? If so, you might just have intellectual property worth protecting.

Is copyright protection automatic? Registering copyright for works you think will be valuable is always a good idea. Although you do have copyright without registration, registering your copyright provides certain advantages, as shown in the table in Figure 1.19.

Advantages (Per the U.S. Copyright Office)	Explanation
Registration establishes a public record of the copyright claim.	Much harder for someone to argue they were unaware your material was copyrighted. Can make it easier for a person or entity to locate you and request permission to use your work.
Before an infringement suit may be filed in court, registration is necessary for works of U.S. origin.	You can sue someone for infringement and recover damages.
If registration is made within three months after publication of the work or prior to an infringement of the work, statutory damages and attorney's fees will be available to the copyright owner in court actions.	Without timely registration, only actual damages can be recovered.
Registration allows the owner of the copyright to record the registration with the U.S. Customs Service for protection against the importation of infringing copies.	Important for protecting your work—especially CDs and DVDs—from being infringed upon by people pirating copies from overseas.

Figure 1.19
Advantages of registering copyright.

How do you register work for copyright protection? Instructions and forms for registering work for copyright protection can be found on the U.S. Copyright Office Web site at *www.copyright.gov*. Registration can be done online and requires the payment of a small fee ($35 at time of publication). Although you can file online, the Library of Congress might still require you to submit a hard copy of your work. It can take quite a while to receive your notice of registration (up to eight months), but your registration is effective when the Copyright Office receives your registration form.

Posting a copyright notice with your work is also a great deterrent to copyright infringement as it clearly establishes the work is copyrighted. A simple format is to use the word copyright (or the copyright symbol—©), the year the work was first published, the copyright holder's name, and optionally, the location of the copyright holder. For example, either of these notifications for this book would be appropriate:

Copyright 2010 Pearson Education, Inc., Upper Saddle River, NJ

or

© 2010 Pearson Education, Inc.

Will it cost $35 to register each picture if there are 400 pictures? A copyright registration form can be filed for a collection of works. The stipulation is that the works must be published as a collection. A group of images or a collection of blog postings published online prior to registration should meet this criterion.

Can government copyright records be searched to determine if a work is copyrighted? The records are open to the public, and records from 1978 forward are searchable in an online database, as shown in Figure 1.20. For a search of records prior to January 1, 1978, you need to take a trip to Washington, DC, and do the search yourself in the paper records or pay the Copyright Office $150 per hour to conduct a search for you. Because the personnel at the copyright office are probably more proficient at searching than you are, a paid search is often the best option.

Online searching is available for works published after 1977.

Instructions for paper file searches are detailed by following this link.

Figure 1.20
Begin your copyright search online or find out how to search offline at *www.copyright.gov/records*.

What if the creator of the work doesn't mind people using it but doesn't want to be hassled constantly by permission requests?
Copyleft—a play on the word copyright—is designed for this situation. Copyright laws are designed to allow copyright holders to prevent other people from copying, modifying, or distributing the creator's work. Copyleft is a term for various licensing plans that enable copyright holders to grant

certain rights to the work while retaining other rights. Usually, the rights (such as modifying or copying a work) are granted with the stipulation that when users redistribute their work (based upon the original work) they agree to be bound by the same terms of the copyleft plan used by the original copyright holder. The General Public License (GNU) is a popular copyleft license that is used for software. For other works, the Creative Commons, a non-profit organization, has developed a range of licenses that can be used to control rights to works.

Creative Commons (see Figure 1.21) has various types of licenses available based on the rights you want to grant. The company—located on the Web at *www.creativecommons.org/about/licenses*—provides a simple form to assist you with selecting the proper license for your work and the following licenses you can choose from:

- **Attribution**—This condition lets others "copy, distribute, display, and perform your copyrighted work—and derivative works based upon it—but only if they give credit the way you request."

- **Noncommercial**—This condition lets others "copy, distribute, display, and perform your work—and derivative works based upon it—but for noncommercial purposes only."

- **No Derivative Works**—This condition lets others "copy, distribute, display, and perform only verbatim copies of your work, not derivative works based upon it."

- **Share Alike**—This condition lets others "distribute derivative works only under a license identical to the license that governs your work."

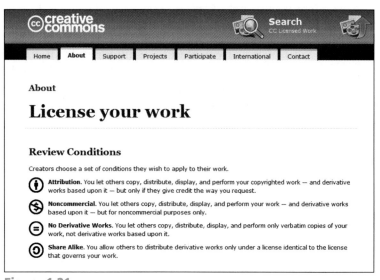

Figure 1.21
The Creative Commons Web site.

What are the advantages and drawbacks of licenses designed by Creative Commons? The obvious advantage is that people won't hassle you with endless permission requests. They should know exactly how you are willing to have your work be used. Also, many advocates of copyleft schemes feel that creativity is encouraged when people are free to modify others' work instead of worrying about infringing on copyright.

Opponents of Creative Common's licenses often complain that these licenses have affected their livelihoods. With millions of images out on Flickr with Creative Common's licenses that permit free commercial use, professional photographers might have a tougher time selling their work. Also Creative Common's licenses are irrevocable. If you made a mistake and selected the wrong license for your work or you later find out a work is valuable and you've already selected a license that allows commercial use, you're out of luck. Also, many people find Creative Common's licenses confusing. If there is a Creative Commons disclaimer at the bottom of a blog, does that mean all the blog entries apply to that license or just some of them? What actually constitutes commercial use? Is displaying Google Adsense ads on your blog commercial use?

You need to carefully consider the value of your intellectual property and decide how best to protect your rights. You should proceed carefully before giving up some of your rights with any copyleft license, especially if it is irrevocable.

Objective 10
Define Plagiarism

Is plagiarism a form of copyright infringement? *Plagiarism* is the act of copying text or ideas from someone else and claiming them as your own work product. Using ideas from other sources and integrating them into your work is acceptable only if you disclose your source and identify the content you use with quotation marks. Changing a few words, but keeping the essence of someone else's idea is still plagiarism even if you don't copy the text exactly. Although the following examples don't involve copying words or ideas without attribution, they are still examples of plagiarism under the academic definition:

- **Turning in work that someone else did for you**—Copying the Excel file that was due for homework in your computer literacy class from a classmate is still plagiarism, even though the file is not a text file.

- **Failing to identify a quotation with quotation marks**—"Whoops, I forgot" is not a suitable defense!

- **Falsifying quotations or sources**—Sometimes, students feel that attributing an idea of their own to a highly regarded source makes their idea sound more credible. Students have been known to enhance a paper that is thin on research sources by adding a list of sources and attributing them to various parts of the document.

- **Copying too much material from other sources**—If a work consists mostly of quotes and ideas from other sources, even though the source has been identified, it is difficult to justify this as original, creative work.

Plagiarism is usually considered an academic offense of dishonesty and is not punishable under U.S. civil law. However, it certainly is prohibited by almost all academic institutions, and the penalties usually are severe, such as a failing grade on the assignment, a failing grade for the course, or being dismissed from the institution. Although plagiarism is not technically copyright infringement, it can easily turn into copyright infringement if too much material is stolen from other sources, such as an entire chapter of a book or an entire research paper.

Why does plagiarism get so much press today when it has been a problem for centuries? Unfortunately, quick access to volumes of information on the Internet has made it easier than ever to commit plagiarism. Just a few clicks of the mouse can copy large quantities of information. Essay paper mills are Web sites that sell prewritten or custom written research papers to students. The essays are often written by graduate students or professional ghostwriters. For custom work, you can even specify what type of grade you would like to get. Some students choose to buy papers to earn them a grade of "C" if they think that it is less likely to arouse suspicion from the professor. Although it is illegal in most states to sell essays that will be turned in by students as their own work, the mills get around this by putting disclaimers on their Web sites that the papers should be used only for research purposes and not as the student's own work. Fortunately, there are good tools available to professors for detecting this type of plagiarism.

What can professors do to detect plagiarism? Sometimes, just reading a student's work product is a dead giveaway. If the level of writing suddenly improves dramatically from earlier assignments, most professors immediately become suspicious. Most colleges allow professors to test students orally on the content of papers that they suspect are not the student's own work product. If a student is unfamiliar with the content of the paper and the sources used, charges of academic dishonesty are usually brought against the student.

Typing suspicious phrases from a paper into Google and searching for hits is also an effective way to find unaccredited sources. Often, the plagiarized material turns up in the first page of Google results so professors don't even have to search hard to discover it. Also, most school libraries subscribe to online, searchable databases of periodicals that contain the full text of published articles. This aids professors in ferreting out plagiarism from printed sources.

Because of rampant plagiarism in recent decades, specialized electronic tools such as turnitin.com have been developed. Turnitin.com is a Web site to which educational institutions subscribe. The subscription enables professors to upload student papers, which are then checked against Web pages from the Internet—both current pages and archived pages that are no longer live—student papers previously submitted to Turnitin, and databases of published journals and periodicals. Customized reports, such as the one shown in Figure 1.22, are generated to determine the amount of suspected plagiarism in the paper. Professors also have the option of letting students upload their papers and check them for inadvertent plagiarism to give them a chance to cite unaccredited sources before turning in their final product.

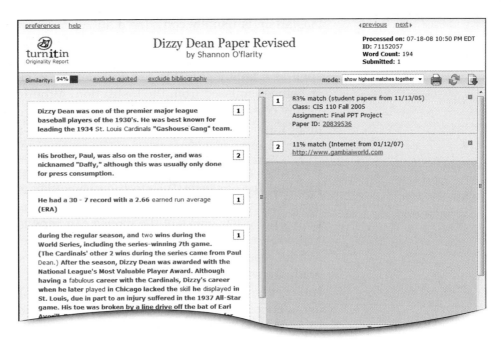

Figure 1.22
The turnitin.com originality report for this paper clearly shows that most of the paper was plagiarized from one turned in previously by another student with some small additions that were directly lifted from the Internet.

Why do students plagiarize? There are many reasons that students commit plagiarism. These include:

- **Pressure and deadlines outside of school**—Students, especially community college students, have a lot going on in their lives besides schoolwork. Often students are juggling jobs, family responsibilities, and relationships with their friends. Sometimes, they run out of time to get everything accomplished. This pressure to meet a deadline often results in a student taking the easy way out—plagiarism.

- **Poor time management and lack of advanced planning**—Many students have trouble assessing the amount of work that is necessary to complete an assignment. Coupled with poor management of time and responsibilities, this can lead some students to seek shortcuts to completing an assignment.

- **The feeling that everyone does it**—Certain students are under the impression that plagiarism is rampant and because "everyone else is cheating," they must also cheat to remain competitive. Why spend 15 hours on an assignment and risk an average grade when your friend is copying his work and getting As?

- **Perception of poor writing skills**—Many students feel that the sources they are consulting for research express thoughts and ideas much more eloquently than they are able to do. However, the only way to improve your writing skills is to write! Most instructors would rather see a paper that expresses a student's ideas passionately with a few grammar mistakes rather than see work that is stolen from others.

How can I avoid committing plagiarism? Learn to follow this simple maxim: *When in doubt, cite your source.* If you are taking an exact quote from a work, cite the source. If you are paraphrasing someone else's idea but still maintaining the essence of their original, creative idea, cite the source.

How do I cite a printed source properly? There are many different styles of citations you can use that have been developed by organizations such as the American Psychological Association (APA) and the Modern Language Association (MLA). Be sure to ask your professor which style is preferred and ask for relevant examples. Regardless of the style, your objective is to make sure that readers of your work have enough information to find the sources that you cite in your work. In Figure 1.23, you can see the important information to be included in your citation.

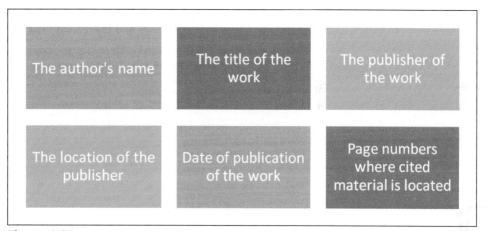

Figure 1.23
Information to include in a citation from a printed work.

How does citing a source from the Internet differ from citing a printed source? Depending on the citation style you are using, there are specific formats to follow that delineate what information to include and exactly how to present it. Regardless of the style being used, you usually need to obtain at least the following information for your citation:

- Author's name.

- Title of the Web page or the title of the Web site if you are citing the entire site.

- Date of creation or revision of the Web site. Note that the dates are usually shown directly under the title, at the top or bottom of the page. If the date is not provided, you can leave this information out of your citation.

- The full *uniform resource locator (URL)*—the Web address—of the Web page.

- The date the Web page or site was accessed. This is the date on which you viewed the Web page. Be sure to keep a record of this as you do research because Web pages can change frequently.

Figure 1.24 provides an example of the pertinent information to gather from an article on a Web site. Keep in mind that this information does not necessarily appear in the same place on every Web page so you may have to look around to find it.

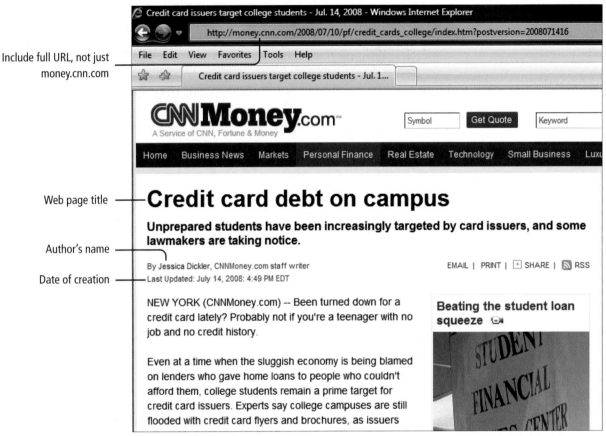

Include full URL, not just money.cnn.com

Web page title

Author's name

Date of creation

Figure 1.24
Relevant information used in Web page citations should be easy to locate. Don't forget to note the date you accessed the Web page.

Remember to properly cite your sources and don't use too much material from published sources. Being proud of your own work and respecting the work of others should keep everyone happy—especially when it comes to the grade you will receive on your work!

End-of-Chapter Assessments

Summary

In this chapter, you learned what ethics are and how your personal ethics develop. You explored various methods for making ethical choices. You learned how to determine which ethical guidelines to follow in a given situation and how to research the guidelines that various institutions (such as your school or your employer) have established. The concepts of intellectual property and copyright protection were explained. You examined the various permissible uses of copyrighted material and learned how to properly request permission to use copyrighted material. The consequences of copyright infringement were evaluated. The concept of fair use was defined and the extent to which it protects students and educators was explored. The various methods available to protect your copyrighted work were explained. Finally, you learned what plagiarism is and how to avoid committing it by citing your sources.

Key Terms

End-of-Chapter Assessments

Matching

Match each term in the second column with its correct definition in the first column by writing the letter of the term on the blank line in front of the correct definition.

_____ **1.** Criteria by which you make ethical decisions.

_____ **2.** General unwritten rules that guide people's behavior.

_____ **3.** People or entities affected by business decisions.

_____ **4.** Ethical guidelines that involve the use of computer systems and the Internet.

_____ **5.** Expressing an opinion in an online forum with strong emotions.

_____ **6.** Property that is an expression of human creativity.

_____ **7.** Legal protection for works of original authorship.

_____ **8.** Defines how you may use copyrighted material.

_____ **9.** Ability to use a portion of a work without obtaining permission.

_____ **10.** Passing off another's ideas as your own.

A Copyright

B Cyberethics

C Fair use

D Flaming

E Intellectual property

F Personal ethics

G Plagiarism

H Societal ethics

I Stakeholders

J Terms of use

End-of-Chapter Assessments

Fill in the Blank

Write the correct answer in the space provided.

1. The _____ gives you the right to resell your text book or loan it to a friend even though you don't own the copyright.

2. Works that lack copyright protection are said to be in the _____.

3. Many Web sites list _____, which delineate the rights you have to use copyrighted work you download from the site.

4. For permission to use a quote from a book, you should contact the _____ or the _____.

5. _____ occurs when you use copyrighted material without first obtaining the copyright holder's permission.

6. Textual URLs pointing to a Web site do not constitute copyright infringement because the URL is deemed to be a _____, which cannot be copyrighted.

7. _____ is a common method of infringement for music and video and involves two computers running common software to swap files.

8. Uploading a video of a band performing a song to YouTube without their permission is a violation of their right to control _____.

9. _____ occurs when someone copies a copyrighted software program and gives it to another person to install on another computer.

10. Usually, the _____ owns the copyright to a photo.

11. A _____ constitutes a request to immediately stop an alleged incidence of infringement.

12. You may be able to use a portion of a copyrighted work without receiving permission from the copyright holder under the _____ doctrine.

13. _____ refers to technology in place on CDs, DVDs, or MP3 files that prevents the media from being copied.

14. The granting of certain rights to a work by a copyright holder while retaining other rights is known as _____.

15. Appropriately _____ your source is the best way to protect yourself from plagiarism.

End-of-Chapter Assessments

Multiple Choice

Circle the letter of the item that correctly answers the question.

1. Under current Unites States law, the term of copyright for a work created today lasts:
   a. Forever
   b. Until the author's death
   c. For 75 years from date of creation
   d. For the life of the author plus 70 years

2. Which of the following has an effect on the development of a person's personal ethics?
   a. Religious affiliation
   b. Influences of family members
   c. Daily life experiences
   d. All of the above

3. Which of the following are not business stakeholders?
   a. Employees
   b. Competitors
   c. Society
   d. Financial lenders

4. Unethical people sometimes find it easier to get away with their behavior on the Internet because of:
   a. The anonymity of online identities
   b. Ease of information exchange
   c. Impersonal nature of electronic communication
   d. All of the above
   e. None of the above

5. The collection of conventions for communicating and exchanging information over the various Internet services is known as:
   a. Cyberethics
   b. Cyber-road rules
   c. Netiquette
   d. Surfing etiquette

6. Which of the following is not an example of intellectual property?
   a. The design for the fastest motorboat in the world
   b. The latest iPod
   c. The theme song NBC played during the Olympics
   d. A poem about trees

(Multiple Choice–continues on the next page)

End-of-Chapter Assessments

Multiple Choice

(Multiple Choice–continued)

7. Which of the following does not constitute intellectual property?
   a. The music contained on a CD
   b. The art on the box containing a DVD of *Spiderman 4*
   c. A DVD of *Spiderman 4*
   d. A poem published in a local newspaper

8. Which of the following cannot be granted copyright protection?
   a. The architectural plans for the new sports stadium to be built in your town
   b. The invention of a new interface for the Apple iPod
   c. A play written by your drama professor
   d. The picture you took last week of your cat

9. The Nike swoosh is an example of a:
   a. Service mark
   b. Trademark
   c. Copyright
   d. Patent

10. When does copyright protection begin?
   a. When a work is published
   b. When a work is registered
   c. When a work is created and fixed in a physical form
   d. When a work is first thought of in someone's mind

Outcome-Based Assessments

End-of-Chapter Exercises

Apply the objectives in this chapter by answering the following questions:

1. What (or who) had the biggest influence on your personal ethics? Are there circumstances that you think you would face during the course of your life that would compel you to make choices that went against your core ethical beliefs?

2. Describe something that one of your friends or coworkers did (no names please!) that was not illegal but that you consider to be unethical. Did this person's actions become public knowledge and did they suffer any negative consequence from the action? Could you ever envision any circumstances in which you would do the same thing they did even though you believe it is fundamentally unethical?

3. You catch the company cleaning staff dumping your employer's garbage into another company's trash dumpster. Your boss asks you to "look the other way" because he told the cleaning staff to take this action in order to cut down on your company's trash hauling expenses. Since there is no legal ordinance in your township prohibiting this action, your boss tells you that "no one is at risk of getting hurt." Explain how you feel about your boss's actions. What would you do in this situation? What possible risks does your company and its employees face even though the action is not illegal?

4. You (lead singer), your roommate (lead guitar), and two of his friends (bass player and drummer) form a band. You and your roommate co-write a song called *College Rocks* for the band. The entire band records the song.
- Who owns copyright to *College Rocks*?
- What rights do the copyright holder(s) have to *College Rocks*?
- The bass player leaves the band and joins another band. Does he have a right to perform *College Rocks* with his new band? Can the new band sell t-shirts with the lyrics to *College Rocks* on it?

5. You find a really cool photo of a woman riding an ostrich on Flickr and download it to your computer. There was no copyright information attached to the photo or displayed on the page of Flickr where you obtained the photo. You are planning on modifying it by using Photoshop to combine it with a photo you have of yourself on a bicycle so it looks like you are chasing the woman. Then you plan to print the modified photo on baseball caps that will be sold at a local rodeo. Consider the following and fully explain your answers:
- Who do you think owns the copyright to the unmodified photo? How would you find out?
- Do you own the copyright to the modified photo?

(End-of-Chapter Exercises—continues on the next page)

(End-of-Chapter Exercises–continued)

- Could you be sued for copyright infringement by the copyright holder of the picture of the woman? If not, explain why. If you could be sued, what types of damages could the copyright holder potentially get from you?
- What if you donated the proceeds of the sales from the hats to charity? Would that change your answer to the previous question?

6. How would you find out if the book *Watership Down* written by British author Richard Adams is in the public domain? If you have an idea for a sequel to *Watership Down* featuring some of the same characters as the original, explain how you could write and publish it without committing copyright infringement.

7. Lucinda works for the Fun Stuff Advertising Agency as an ad copywriter. In her spare time, she is an avid artist. One day her boss tells her the art department has a backlog of work and asks her to design a logo for the Fizzy Cola ad campaign she is currently working on. Lucinda creates the logo on her company owned computer and it is a big hit with the client. The logo is featured in a nationwide television and print advertising campaign for Fizzy Cola. Describe the pertinent facts that must be considered to determine who owns the copyright to the logo: Fun Stuff, Fizzy Cola, or Lucinda.

8. You take a photograph of several students playing with a Frisbee on the quad at Humongous State University (HSU). A classmate of yours is a summer intern at an ad agency who is working on a new ad campaign for Mattel Toys, who markets Frisbees. Your classmate shows the picture around the office and decides it would be good to use in the ad campaign. The representative from Mattel loves it, and it is used in print ads across the United States including a billboard down the street from the college. The week after the billboard appears the following happens:

- You receive a cease and desist letter from HSU indicating that you did not have permission to photograph the college library which appears in the background of the picture.
- You receive a letter from the attorney of one of the students in the picture indicating you are being sued for violating the privacy rights of the student.

Based on what you have read in this book and by doing a little extra research on the Internet (if necessary), explain the legal principles governing each of these situations, what you should have done to avoid being involved in the situations, and whether these complaints have any legal merit.

chapter two

Privacy and Other Ethics Issues

OBJECTIVES

At the end of this chapter you will be able to:

1. Define Privacy and the Associated Risks in Cyberspace
2. Describe the Ethical and Legal Issues of Employee Monitoring
3. Define Cyberbullying and Describe Methods for Mitigation
4. Describe Major Threats to Online Privacy and Methods to Combat the Threats
5. Define E-waste and Describe Methods for Disposing of E-waste
6. Describe Web Content Filtering and Its Effect on Free Speech
7. Define the Digital Divide and Describe Methods for Bridging It
8. Describe Methods to Evaluate the Accuracy of Digital Information
9. Define Online Reputation and Describe Methods for Protecting Your Online Reputation

Introduction

Two of the major ethical issues in cyberspace are violation of digital assets copyright, such as software and
movies, and plagiarism. However, there are many more
ethical choices that users of the Internet are faced with
every day.

In this chapter, you will explore the ethical ramifications of violating privacy rights, such as employers monitoring the behavior of employees, and methods you can
take to protect your privacy rights from being violated by
unethical individuals. In addition, we explore other important ethical issues such as the generation and disposal of
e-waste, assurance of equal access to cyberspace resources
for everyone—bridging the digital divide—and Web content
filtering that restricts access to information.

Objective 1
Define Privacy and the Associated Risks in Cyberspace

Every day it seems like we encounter another issue regarding the disposition of private information in some sector of cyberspace. Perhaps it is a news item about people in your community suffering financial losses from having their identities stolen. Maybe you have heard about the latest data breach from a government agency that allowed supposedly secure data to be accessed by a hacker. Or, maybe you were surprised when the grocery clerk at the supermarket called you by name even though you had never seen him before.

Consider the effect cyberspace has on your day-to-day life. Back in the 1980s, most people paid for purchases with cash. Today, debit and credit cards have largely replaced cash. But whereas cash leaves virtually no trail, a record of your debit and credit card transactions can exist in multiple companies' records. E-mail, text messaging, social networking, and other forms of electronic communication are now the norm. Because of the persistence of digital information, your correspondence may be stored somewhere on the Internet, such as in multiple computers, for years to come. The last time you visited your favorite Web site, the owner of that site probably kept track of what you looked at while you were visiting. Events constantly transpire to make you wonder if privacy is a casualty of the information age.

What is privacy? Simply stated, ***privacy*** is the right to be left alone to do as one pleases as long as there is not a violation of laws or harming of others. Information privacy means that information is controlled in terms of the manner and time frame in which it is disclosed to others. If you worship owls in your living room, perhaps you don't want your neighbors to know this because they might think you strange. However, you may choose to share your views with other owl worshipers because you know they would understand your interest in owls. As long as you aren't hurting the owls—there are laws against cruelty to animals, keeping endangered species, and so on—you should have the right to keep your personal preferences confidential. Someone who obtains or reveals personal information without your consent is said to have committed an ***invasion of privacy***.

Isn't privacy a basic right guaranteed to all Americans? Many Americans think that individual privacy is protected by the Constitution or the Bill of Rights. Our forefathers didn't specifically address the right to individual privacy; however, the Fourth Amendment to the Constitution does reference the right of people to be "secure." The Fourth Amendment states:

"The right of the people to be secure in their persons, houses, papers, and effects, against unreasonable searches and seizures, shall not be violated and no Warrants shall issue, but upon probable cause, supported by Oath or affirmation, and particularly describing the place to be searched, and the persons or things to be seized."

This provision against "unreasonable search and seizure" by government entities as interpreted by the courts, has been interpreted by U.S. society to a reasonable expectation of privacy in any place that is not public or subject to public view. This would include your home and places designed to ensure privacy, such as a public bathroom stall or a phone booth. The right to privacy is a societal norm in the United States. Therefore, it is unethical to violate someone's privacy without his consent.

Can you modify your behavior to protect your privacy? You can modify your behavior to protect your privacy, but would you want to? Would you rather carry cash that can be stolen instead of a debit card that needs a password to be used? For example, do you want to stop purchasing items on the Internet? The electronic exchange and tracking of information makes our lives easier in that it enables us to purchase items without having to leave the comfort of our homes. Tracking activities at a Web site enables the Web site owner to customize the user experience each time the user visits the site. For example, the Amazon Web site makes recommendations to users visiting the site based on the users' previous visits to the site and previous purchases. Only 7 percent of Americans, in a recent poll by the Ponemon Institute (*www.ponemon.org*), said they would be willing to change their behavior to protect their privacy. Although Americans are often vocal about their concerns over loss of privacy, most do not exert pressure on their legislators to enact laws to preserve privacy rights.

Which privacy areas are of concern to most people? Privacy concerns vary widely among individuals. You might not care if your supermarket knows what brand of cereal you buy every week, but your neighbor might consider that a breach of her privacy. The following general types of information are usually of concern to most people:

- **Confidentiality of personal information**—Data such as gender, race, religion, sexual orientation, political affiliation, reading preferences, daily activities, and group memberships are often a source of concern because people want to prevent discrimination, ostracizing, and general embarrassment.

- **Protection of financial information**—Financial information is an area of concern because people want to guard themselves against fraud or identity theft. However, financial transactions can also reveal information about a person's personal life. For example, a company can analyze your purchases through financial transactions.

- **Non-disclosure of medical information**—Most concerns about medical information are related to the ability to obtain insurance or employment. People are also concerned about embarrassment regarding the treatments of certain illnesses. Also, some illnesses might be used correctly or incorrectly to interpret someone's activities or sexual preferences.

In addition to individuals, organizations have valid reasons for maintaining privacy. For example, companies like Coca Cola and other manufacturers often have trade secrets or formulas that they want to protect from falling into the hands of competitors. Some companies might want to keep secret the fact that they participate in an activity that is potentially objectionable to large segments of society. For example, some companies use animal testing for cosmetic products. In these cases, maintaining privacy is a way to avoid adverse or negative publicity.

What ethical responsibilities do you have with regard to privacy? If you are in possession of information about another individual and you do not know whether or not the person would want that information disclosed, you should keep that information confidential. By respecting an individual's right to privacy, you are behaving in an ethical manner.

For example, in the course of employment in a retail clothing store, employees are continually exposed to sensitive information, such as the customers' payment information (credit card numbers), contact information (home or work address and phone numbers), clothing sizes, and even social security numbers. A customer has a reasonable expectation that her credit card numbers will be kept private. You have an "ethical contract" with your customers to protect the information they wish to keep private.

This ethical contract doesn't apply only to employment situations. If your friend John was drunk and made a fool of himself at a small dinner party at your home, you need to respect John's privacy and not describe his antics on your MySpace page. Ethical responsibility regarding privacy is mostly a matter of thinking before acting. Consider if it was you who acted silly. Would you want someone describing you dancing on the top of a table with a t-shirt tied around your head as a bandana after your hometown baseball team just won the World Series? Although your friends might think it was amusing and you might get over your embarrassment relatively quickly, how would a prospective employer feel about your antics? How about your parents? Don't you have a right to privacy when attending a private party in the confines of a friend's home? Put yourself in the other individual's position before you disclose personal or embarrassing information.

Objective 2
Describe the Ethical and Legal Issues of Employee Monitoring

What do employers monitor? Think you aren't being closely watched by your employer? Think again! There are few privacy laws related to the workplace, and most recent court cases tend to support the employer's capability to monitor their employees. A 2005 survey by the American Management Association and the ePolicy Institute (*www.epolicyinstitute .com*) showed that of the employers surveyed, they monitored the following:

- 73% monitored e-mail messages
- 66% monitored Web surfing
- 48% monitored with video surveillance
- 45% monitored keystrokes and keyboard time
- 43% monitored computer files in some other fashion

You need to think carefully about what you are doing at work and what you want your employer to know about because there is a high probability that your employer watches your activities.

Why do employers monitor employees? The two main reasons are to prevent theft—including **industrial espionage**, which is spying by competitors to gain access to sensitive information, and other forms of **white collar crime**, which are non-violent crimes committed by office workers such as fraud, bribery, and stock manipulation—and to measure productivity. Monitoring for theft isn't new because television cameras have been around for years, and productivity monitoring has been a consistent process for assembly line workers for decades. The rise of the Internet has enabled a new type of productivity drain.

Cyberloafing, or cyberslacking, is doing anything with a computer—usually involving the Internet—on company time that is not related to your job while you are being paid to do your job. Examples of cyberloafing activities are surfing the Web, playing games, reading personal e-mail, running another business, such as an eBay business, and watching videos. Estimates of business productivity losses due to cyberloafing top $50 billion annually. Although many employers don't mind the occasional personal e-mail answered at work, they would probably not appreciate it if you spent four hours of your day playing *World of Warcraft* online (see Figure 2.1)!

Figure 2.1
Your boss may be watching to ensure your honesty and productivity.

Do I have a legal right (in the United States) to a reasonable expectation of privacy in the workplace? The 1986 Electronic Communications Privacy Act (ECPA) is the federal law that most closely applies to privacy in the workplace. Among the provisions of the act are prohibitions against the unauthorized monitoring of electronic communications, which includes e-mail. The law specifically exempts *service providers* from its provisions, and the courts have interpreted this to mean employers who routinely provide electronic communication services such as Internet access, e-mail, and cellular phone texting service. When cases have come to court, the court's view is usually that because the employer is paying for the equipment and software, the employees don't have an expectation of privacy that they could easily enjoy by communicating on their own time with their own electronic devices.

Shouldn't people be allowed some privacy at work? Many employees feel that an employer should allow some leeway during the day to take care of personal business that can be conducted only during normal work hours. With the lengthening of the U.S. work week over the past several decades, this is not an unreasonable expectation. But the allowances an employer will make vary widely from employer to employer. You need to understand the difference between acceptable and unacceptable conduct at your place of business. And even though your employer might allow you to do some personal tasks during the day, it doesn't mean those tasks won't be monitored.

Is it ethical for employers to monitor employees? Just because an action is legal doesn't mean it is ethical. It is difficult to argue that an employer doesn't have the right to take measures to prevent theft and detect low productivity. The ethical issue here is whether or not the employees are made aware they are being monitored. An ethical employer should treat employees with respect and dignity and inform the employees that they are being monitored. Also, employers have an ethical responsibility—a legal one, too, depending on the jurisdiction—to not place monitoring devices in sensitive locations such as bathrooms and dressing areas.

Do employers have a legal obligation to notify employees they are being monitored? In most cases—although it can vary from state to state—the employer does not need to inform the employees in advance that they are being monitored. However, most employers include this in published employee policies to avoid confusion and conflict. If you aren't sure if your employer monitors employees, check with the human resources department at your employer.

Can an employer monitor employee phone calls? Yes, an employer can monitor phone calls as long as they are business-related. The ECPA specifically exempts personal calls from monitoring so if your employer monitors your calls, they are supposed to stop when they realize you are making a personal call. Your employer may specifically state that no personal calls are to be made from certain business phones, in which case, you can assume that all calls from those phones are monitored. The number of phone calls, the duration of the calls, and the specific numbers dialed are often reviewed by employers for judging worker productivity. Ten calls per day to a spouse may be noted in a performance review. With the rise of cellular phones, it is easy to maintain your privacy on phone calls at work. Simply make all personal calls on your cell phone.

However, to be fair to your employer, you should keep personal calls at work to a minimum because you are supposed to be working. Spending three hours a day on personal calls does not constitute turning in an honest day's effort!

How are computers monitored? Employers use a variety of software programs to monitor employee computer usage. Certain software packages keep track of every Web site you visit and the duration of your stay. Checking the baseball scores might take only three seconds and go unnoticed, but spending two hours updating your fantasy football team might get flagged. **_Keystroke loggers_** are software packages that record every key stroke you make on your computer. Originally they were used to monitor performance for people with input-intensive jobs like clerks and secretaries. Now these programs can be used to invade your privacy because they record everything you type, even that nasty e-mail about the boss that you thought better of sending and deleted!

In addition to monitoring keystrokes, computer software can also be used to monitor the contents of your hard drive, so you don't want to collect 4,823 illegal MP3 files on your work computer. Some programs even keep track of how long your computer is idle, which can give your manager a good idea of whether you were working or away for a three-hour lunch.

Your employer might not tell you that your computer use is being monitored, so you should assume that anything you do on your company-provided computer is subject to scrutiny. If you need to do personal work on your lunch hour or other breaks, bring in your personal laptop to avoid the monitoring.

Are all my e-mail communications subject to monitoring? E-mail sent from employer-owned systems can be monitored. Also, the courts have indicated that e-mail sent from third-party systems, such as Yahoo and Gmail, are subject to monitoring if they are sent on employer-provided computer systems. Instant messaging is also subject to monitoring. About the only exception to communications monitoring are phone text messages.

In the case of *Quon v. Arch Wireless, et al.* Ninth Circuit, June 18, 2008, No. 07-55282, the 9th U.S. Circuit Court of Appeals ruled in June 2008 that employers can view phone text messages only if they have the employee's permission or a valid legal warrant. The distinction between text messages and e-mail are that the text messages are stored by a third party and that the employer does not directly pay for storage of those messages. E-mail is usually stored on a company-owned server or on a third-party server for which the third party is paid specifically to store the messages.

Again, the best defense against monitoring of personal instant messaging, text messaging or e-mail is to use your own computing device to send the communications.

Figure 2.2
You can save yourself a lot of angst about your communications being monitored in the workplace by using your own cell phone or computer for personal communication.

What protects employees from those who monitor and then misuse personal information? People who monitor employees have a duty to protect your right to privacy and not to disclose any information that they may inadvertently see during the course of monitoring. The acceptable computer use policies at most companies include guidelines for network administrators and other people who have higher levels of access to sensitive information.

In addition to the procedures for preventing abuse of data that is monitored, companies need strong policies to safeguard customer and employee data. Companies need to prevent data theft and loss from happening because these crimes can lead to identity theft. Consider the 2007 theft of the data backup device stolen from a college intern's car. The intern was working for the state of Ohio at the time and the stolen device contained data on 1.3 million taxpayers and employees. Procedures for investigating employee misuse of computers and data and the sanctions that will be imposed for violations must be detailed.

Whether monitoring employees' work habits or safeguarding data, management must ensure that compliance with the policies is tested periodically. Periodic reviews of procedures and compliance helps ensure that established company policies are working as designed. An ethical company strives to prevent misuse of personal data and accidental data loss. This helps the company maintain the trust of its employees, customers, and the public.

Objective 3
Define Cyberbullying and Describe Methods for Mitigation

What is cyberbullying? *Cyberbullying* is just like normal bullying, but it involves the use of digital technologies such as the Internet, cell phones, or video. Instead of a bully chasing you at recess on the playground, cyberbullying involves minors (children) harassing, threatening, humiliating, embarrassing, or tormenting other minors by means of technology. Cyberbullying is not an adult behavior. *Cyber-harassment*—threatening or annoying others in cyberspace—or *cyberstalking*—threatening an individual via electronic communications—are incidents that involve adults. Cyberbullying is a child-on-child process that might result in criminal charges depending upon the type of incident.

How does cyberbullying take place? There are many direct and indirect methods of cyberbullying. The main ones are:

- **Instant messaging or text messaging**—Often groups of children will bombard a victim with thousands of text messages. Sometimes a bully will create an IM account and pretend to be the intended victim and act in such a way as to embarrass or anger the victim's friends.

- **Password theft**—If students discover someone's password, they may log onto their accounts and send harassing, threatening, or lewd messages while pretending to be the victim.

- **Blog and Social Networking sites**—Children often post nasty rumors about other kids on these sites. This exposes the victim to widespread humiliation and embarrassment, especially as other people add comments to postings and start their own rumors. Often these sites feature cruel polls, such as a vote about who is the "fattest" kid in the class.

- **Embarrassing photos or videos**—Usually candid photos or videos—often nude or semi-nude photos that have been taken discretely with cell phone cameras—are sent through cell phones or e-mails. These can circulate widely and end up on Web sites all over the world.

- **Malware**—Computer-savvy cyberbullies often send viruses or Trojan horse programs to their victims in attempts to disable their computers or spy on them.

- **Junk e-mail or text messaging**—Bullies often sign their victims up with hundreds of marketing or porn sites in an attempt to flood their accounts with annoying messages.

Why is cyberbullying unethical? Most bullying involves harassment, spreading of false rumors or revealing embarrassing, personal details about an individual. The individual's right to privacy (just to be left alone and do his own thing) is violated by these actions, which are considered unethical in our society. Children have the same expectations of anonymity when they use Internet services as adults and should respect the privacy of others. Unfortunately, some children fail to treat their peers with respect and behave unethically.

Why does cyberbullying take place? Children are often more trusting than adults and may be more willing to reveal personal information, such as passwords, to their friends. Because younger people are so comfortable using the Internet, they often forget to exercise the same precautions over sensitive information that they would exercise in the real world. And sometimes children just want to fit in with the "popular kids," so they reveal a lot of information about themselves in the hopes of being accepted. Unfortunately, these behaviors make it easier for cyberbullies to commit their unethical activities.

How do cyberbullies typically behave? Although every cyberbullying incident can be slightly different, there are common characteristics that cyberbullies share. According to *www.stopcyberbullying.org*, there are four main categories of cyberbullies:

- **The Vengeful Angel**—These people don't view themselves as bullies but think they are avenging some wrong, protecting a friend, or retaliating against another cyberbully. They often think they are teaching their victim a well-deserved lesson.

- **The Power Hungry (*Revenge of the Nerds*)**—Some bullies like to show off their power or intimidate others through fear. Many of these bullies just want to show how much smarter they are than the intended victim. They enjoy making people feel powerless.

- **Mean Girls**—These bullies, who do not have to be female, are either bored or searching for a cruel form of entertainment. They usually work in groups because they enjoy having an audience for their pranks. Fortunately, these bullies frequently lose interest if they don't get a sufficiently entertaining reaction from their victims.

- **Inadvertent Cyberbully**—These people are not intentionally being cyberbullies, but are usually just thoughtless. They dash off a mean e-mail, IM, or text message and hit send before thinking about the consequences. They frequently respond out of anger or frustration for something that happened to them.

Are the consequences of cyberbullying serious? For many adults, their job and their families define who they are and affect how happy and successful they feel. For children, their standing in peer groups is a critical component of their self worth. Adults have freedom in their lives to change bad situations, such as changing jobs, when they feel their esteem is under attack. Children often feel powerless because they have such limited options. You might have been mortified in sixth grade if someone had sent around a picture of you in your underwear when you were changing in the locker room. Children don't usually have the option of changing schools without uprooting the entire family. Aside from developing severe feelings of depression, rage, frustration, and powerlessness, children have committed suicide over cyberbullying incidents.

How do you overcome cyberbullying? There are no easy answers to overcoming cyberbullying, but educating and informing children about the consequences of cyberbullying are effective solutions. Often, when children are educated about the behaviors of cyberbullies, they recognize that some of the actions they take contain aspects of bullying.

Children need to suffer consequences for their actions, such as having their cell phones taken away if they send thousands of text messages to a cyberbullying victim. Children also need to be educated about the possible effects on their intended victims, such as anger, depression, and even suicide. Programs that teach children to manage their anger—always useful in later life—by stepping back and taking a critical look at situations that enrage them before they act can be effective in preventing cyberbullying incidents. Finally, when someone understands that it is unethical to take a facilitator role in other cyberbullying schemes, they are less inclined to participate, such as not forwarding a hurtful e-mail or making a nasty post on someone's blog.

What can adults do to prevent cyberbullying? Parents need to be alert to changes in their children's behavior which may indicate they are victims of cyberbullying or becoming bullies themselves. If a child is suddenly spending a lot less time or more time online, what is the reason? Is your child suddenly depressed or getting sick frequently to avoid going to school? Maintaining open channels of communication with children is important because they need to be able to inform a trusted adult— parent, teacher, counselor, or religious leader—when they are being harassed or bullied.

Objective 4
Describe Major Threats to Online Privacy and Methods to Combat the Threats

There are many threats to personal privacy from individuals, such as hackers, behaving unethically online. Computer viruses and spyware can cause havoc by disrupting your computing experience or by collecting personal information, such as credit card numbers, to be used in the commission of **cybercrimes**—criminal activities conducted with the aid of a computer or the Internet. Most individuals are aware of these threats and can combat them by using software solutions such as anti-virus programs, anti-spyware programs, and firewalls. Obviously, hacking, creating viruses, and deploying spyware are unethical activities, and we don't expect you to engage in these activities. However, because there are unethical individuals who will attempt to take advantage of you with these methods, you need to know how to protect yourself. In this section, you explore threats to your privacy that require more diligence to defend yourself against. You will also look at suggestions for how to protect your privacy online.

How can I possibly be a threat to myself? People are often too eager to reveal information about themselves, especially when it appears that the request is coming from a legitimate source. Have you filled out a warranty form online for a product you bought lately? Have you obtained a customer loyalty card at a pharmacy or a supermarket? Have you filled out a survey to potentially win a prize? Think about how much information you voluntarily gave up performing these activities. In addition, if you have a MySpace, Facebook, Blogger, or Twitter account, you are probably constantly revealing information about your likes and dislikes—what movie you saw this weekend, which concert you attended last night, presents you received for your birthday, and so on. Con artists and scammers take advantage of this tendency to reveal one's self, and they collect information by using a technique called social engineering.

How does social engineering work? *Social engineering* uses social skills to generate human interaction that leads to individuals revealing sensitive information. Social engineering often doesn't involve the use of a computer or face-to-face interaction. Telephone scams are common because it is often easier to manipulate someone when you don't have to look at them. The two main types of social engineering are as follows:

- *Pretexting*—Pretexting involves creating a scenario that sounds legitimate enough that someone will trust you. For example, you might receive a phone call during which the caller says he is from the bank and that someone tried to use your account without authorization. The caller then tells you he needs to confirm a few personal details such as your birth date, social security number, bank account number, and whatever other information he can get out of you. The information he obtains can then be used to empty your bank account or commit some other form of fraud. Often pretexting is used to gain access to corporate computer networks. People will sometimes call random extensions in a large business claiming to be from technical support. Eventually, the caller will find someone who has a problem and is happy that someone is willing to help. The scam artist will then elicit information such as logons and passwords from the victim as part of the process for "solving the problem."

- *Phishing*—Phishing usually involves sending e-mails—although instant messaging, phone texting, and telephoning can also be used—that appear to come from an official source, such as your bank, eBay, Paypal, and so on. Phishing messages are used to gather sensitive information from unsuspecting individuals. The e-mail, as shown in Figure 2.3, usually gets your attention by mentioning something that might make you upset: unauthorized access to your account, large payments made from your account, and so on. The e-mail might then contain a link to a Web site where you are asked to enter sensitive information about your account, such passwords, social security number, birth date, and so on. The phishing Web site is made to look as close to the official Web site as possible and may even feature logos and text copied directly from the legitimate site. These e-mails are insidious because they often disguise the links to look like the official links of the real organization. In addition, the fake Web sites often use computer programming to alter the address bar in your browser so that it looks like you are on the official site instead of a phishing site.

Ginormous National Bank

Dear Ginormous valued customer:

Recently, Ginormous bank account holders have been the victims of attempt to steal their identity for the purposes of committing fraud and misappropriating funds in bank accounts. In order to protect your account, we are requiring you to change your Ginormous Bank ATM card PIN code.

This notification is not an indication that your account has been compromised. But at Ginormous bank, we take our depositor's security seriously and are taking this action to prevent unauthorized access to your account.

Note the use of scare tactics ————You must take action within seven business days or your account may be temporarily suspended and you may not be able to access your funds.

To update your ATM PIN code, please click on the following link:

Clicking on the link would take you to an official looking page to record your sensitive information. ————http://ginormousbank.com/cgi-bin/atmupdate/fraudprevention/loginpage.asp

We appreciate your prompt attention to this matter and look forward to serving you in the future.

Best regards,
William H. Robinson
Vice President, Fraud Prevention

Figure 2.3
Example of a phishing e-mail from Ginormous National Bank. Obviously, actual phishing attempts appear to be from real financial institutions.

How do you avoid falling for social engineering schemes? Be wary of all unsolicited phone calls when you are being asked for personal information. Hang up and call the appropriate institution (your bank, for example) using a phone number from a source you trust, such as your bank statement, credit card statement, and so on. You will quickly ascertain whether there is an actual problem. Also, never respond to e-mails or click on links they contain, especially in e-mails that are trying to "verify" sensitive information. Bank personnel never send e-mails asking for personal information such as your account number because they already know it! Instead, contact the appropriate institution directly and see if the e-mail is legitimate.

The latest version of the popular Web browsers, such as Internet Explorer and Firefox, contain anti-phishing measures that check Web sites against a database of known phishing sites and warn you if you browse to a suspect site. For additional protection, anti-phishing software comes with most Internet Security Suite software packages such as Norton Internet Security (see Figure 2.4). The Norton Internet Security toolbar will alert you if you browse to a known phishing site. It would be a good idea to purchase a security product that does help protect you against phishing scams.

Norton Internet
Security toolbar

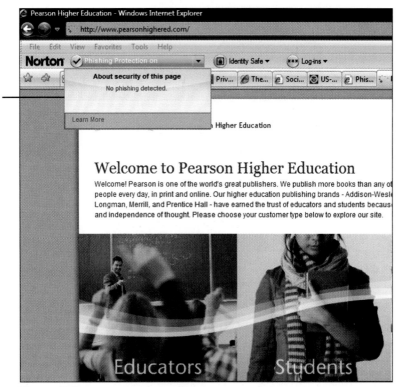

Figure 2.4
Not sure if you are on the real Pearson Higher Education Web site? Norton Internet Security's tool bar gives you added assurance.

What do you do if you think you have fallen victim to a phishing or other social engineering scheme? If you have suspicions of being a victim of phishing or social engineering, immediately contact the appropriate institution—your bank, Paypal, Amazon.com, and so on. Ask for the fraud division and explain what happened. They should be able to freeze your account, assist you in changing passwords, or close your old account and open a new one for you. Don't be embarrassed to call for help; this type of scam fools even seasoned professionals sometimes.

What is identity theft? When someone steals your personal information such as your name, address, social security number, and birth date and then uses that information to impersonate you and run up debts in your name, the crime is known as *identity theft* (see Figure 2.5). The identity thief will usually open new charge accounts in your name or will obtain loans at financial institutions. The first indication that you've been a victim is often not until you receive a charge card bill for items you never bought. Victims of identity theft spend months (and even years) trying to repair their credit and eliminate fraudulent debts.

Figure 2.5
How many people are posing as you? Identity theft can strike at any time!

Some identity thieves use your information to obtain medical services from doctors and hospitals. Identity theft victims have found themselves denied coverage because the thief's treatment sent them over the limit of covered services on their policy. The "2008 Identity Fraud Survey Report" by Javelin Strategy & Research reported that approximately 8.1 million American adults were victims of identity theft in 2007. Clearly, this is widespread problem against which you need to protect yourself.

How do identities get stolen? Many people believe that identity theft happens only through computers, but this is untrue. The "2008 Identity Fraud Survey Report" indicates that identity theft fraud through telephone and conventional mail tactics accounts for approximately 40 percent of identity theft. The U.S. Federal Trade Commission (*www.ftc.gov*) lists the following sources of identity theft that have nothing to do with computers or electronic data:

- **Theft of purses and wallets**—Many people carry valuable personal information such as their ATM PIN codes or social security cards. You should memorize both these numbers; do not carry them in your wallet.

- **Dumpster diving**—Thieves dig through trash to find bank statements and credit card bills, which often provide valuable personal information.

- **Pretexting**—Posing as bank or credit card company representatives often enables thieves to fool people into revealing personal information by phone.

Of course you are at risk from online attacks also. For example, responding to phishing e-mails often results in you handing over your information voluntarily.

What else do identity thieves do with my information? Although creative identity thieves can do numerous nasty things, the most common are:

- Request a change of address with financial institutions—The thief cleans out your bank account or maxes out your credit limit before you realize you aren't receiving statements.

- Open bank accounts in your name and write bad checks—This ruins your credit rating.

- Obtain a mortgage in your name to purchase real estate—not necessarily the home in which you live—and then disappear with the proceeds, leaving you with the debt. This can be the toughest problem to repair.

How do you protect yourself against identity theft? It is impossible to fully protect yourself against identity theft but taking the following steps can decrease your risk of being a victim:

- Never reveal passwords, logon IDs, and PIN codes to anyone. Don't write them down and leave them in an easily accessible place. If you need to write them down because you just can't remember them, put the list in your safe deposit box at the bank.

- Think carefully before giving out personal information, especially online. Only give information that a company needs (for example, retail stores don't need your social security number or your birth date to sell you a television or pair of jeans).

- Don't respond to requests for personal information when someone calls you. Hang up and call the company directly to verify that the call is legitimate.

- Create secure passwords for your accounts. Combinations of letters, numbers, and symbols work best. For example, IUX34#WS7 is a strong password. Thieves are adept at guessing obvious passwords such as names, and even your pets' names, birth dates, portions of social security numbers, your address, and so on.

- Shop only with well-known online merchants. Check with the Better Business Bureau before dealing with a merchant for the first time to see if they have complaints lodged against them. Businesses should have valid contact information on their Web site such as a mailing address and phone number.

- Most states now allow you to freeze your credit history. This prevents anyone from checking your credit, including you, through the three main credit bureaus, and legitimate merchants won't open a new charge account without a credit check. You can always unfreeze your credit later if you need to apply for a loan.

For additional tips on preventing identity theft or for procedures to follow if you are a victim, check out the U.S. federal government site on identity theft at *www.consumer.gov/idtheft*.

What other steps can you take to maintain your online anonymity and privacy? Aside from the obvious steps of not giving out personal information and not identifying yourself on social networking sites and other Web pages, you should take the following steps:

- **Restrict access to your online information**—You may have good reasons for creating an account under your real name at Facebook or LinkedIn, such as networking to find a better job. But that doesn't mean you have to let everyone see your information. Check the options and restrict all or part of your account to just your trusted friends.

- **Exercise caution when using public terminals or networks**—The computer at the student union or the wireless network at the local coffee shop are convenient. That doesn't necessarily mean they are secure. Information thieves often hang around in places that offer public computer access—such as libraries—because people often leave a trail of information behind when they surf the Internet. You never know what monitoring software hackers may have installed on a public computer. Likewise, open wireless networks in public places offer hackers a chance to intercept messages you send and to possibly steal sensitive information such as credit card numbers. Therefore, when using public computers and wireless networks, you should take the following steps:

  - When you use a public computer at school, the library, and so on, always make sure you log out of all the accounts you accessed and close your browser.

  - Do not make financial transactions on public computers or open wireless networks.

  - Consider using portable privacy devices like the IronKey (*www.ironkey.com*), shown in Figure 2.6. The device plugs into a USB port on the computer you use. Instead of being stored on the computer, all sensitive files, such as cookies, Internet history (list of Web sites you have visited), and browser caches (copies of Web pages you surfed), are stored on the privacy device. Therefore, you don't leave an electronic trail for hackers to follow on the public computer. Many of these privacy devices use software such as the Anonymizer Safe Surfing Suite (*www.anonymizer.com*), which shields your Internet address from prying eyes. This makes it difficult or impossible for hackers to tell where you are surfing on the Internet. Password management tools are included with these devices so you can store logon information easily. The data is encrypted so even if you lose the device, your information should remain safe.

Figure 2.6
Products such as the IronKey help to protect your privacy when working on computers away from your home or office.

- **Create Strong Passwords**—Well-constructed passwords are difficult to guess and contain a combination of upper and lowercase letters, numbers, and symbols (such as # or &). The ideal length for secure passwords is at least 12 characters. Strong passwords do not contain dictionary words, letter or number sequences, such as 1234 or ABCD, or personal information, such as birth dates, street addresses, names of your pets, and so on. You should avoid using the same password for all the Web sites that you access to make it more difficult for thieves if they obtain one of your passwords. Web sites such as *www.passwordmeter.com* (see Figure 2.7) can help you evaluate the strength of your passwords.

Enter your password here ——

Evaluation of strength ——

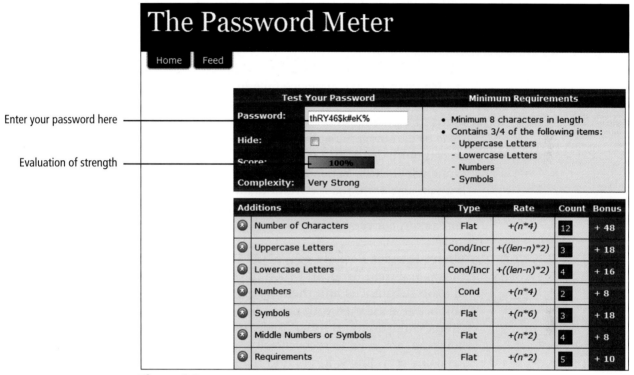

Figure 2.7
The Password Meter gives you a free evaluation of the strength of your password.

- **Change your passwords frequently**—You should change your passwords on a regular basis to improve your security. However, strong passwords that you constantly change can be challenging to remember. Therefore, you may want to use password management software to keep track of your passwords. Windows Vista, the Firefox browser, and security products (such as Norton 360) all have password management tools. The software stores all of your passwords for you to make logging onto your favorite Web sites a breeze. Even though you have different passwords for each site, you'll need to remember only one master password for the password management software to gain access to all your passwords.

Protecting your privacy requires the use of vigilance, common sense, and appropriate software programs. Enjoy the Internet, but practice caution to maintain your anonymity and privacy.

Objective 5
Define E-waste and Describe Methods for Disposing of E-waste

Did you ever throw away an old cell phone because it stopped working? Perhaps you bought a new computer and put your old one out on the sidewalk for trash collection. What will you do with your iPod when the battery no longer holds a charge? Replace the battery or get a newer iPod? All of these decisions impact a growing world problem of the disposal of electronic waste or e-waste.

What is e-waste and why is it a problem? Any broken or discarded electronic or electrical device falls in the category of *e-waste*. E-waste is much more difficult to dispose of or recycle than normal waste because many of the components of e-waste are not biodegradable or contain toxic or carcinogenic substances. E-waste can include substances such as cadmium, lead, and mercury—all highly toxic—and polychlorinated biphenyls (PCBs), which are known carcinogens. The problem is that e-waste also contains recoverable metals, such as gold, silver, and copper, whose prices are rising on the world market. This makes e-waste a valuable commodity for recycling.

Where is most e-waste recycled? Unfortunately, because the United States and the European Union have stringent laws about the handling of toxic substances and their disposal, much of the world's e-waste is shipped to countries with much less stringent pollution laws, such as China, Pakistan, and India. Risky methods, such as plastic and copper smelting, are used to recover valuable resources from the waste while exposing recycling workers and the surrounding environment to unsafe levels of toxic substances. The components that can't be recycled— mostly non-biodegradable—end up in landfills in developing countries. Although you could argue that the developing countries doing the recycling receive economic benefit, it can easily be argued that developed countries dumping their toxic wastes on less developed countries is unethical. Remember that analyzing the ethics of a situation involves considering whether a decision is fair to all involved. Is it fair for developed countries to use developing countries as their trash dump?

What can I do about the problem of e-waste? The main thing you can do is generate less e-waste, which sounds like an obvious solution. Use products for as long as possible by upgrading or refurbishing them. Do you need a brand new iPod when you can replace the battery pack in your old one? A 50-inch plasma TV sounds great until you consider discarding an old television that still works.

Donating products that you no longer need, but that still work, to someone who can use them is another great solution. Many manufacturers of electronic products provide resources on their Web sites for locating organizations to which you can donate your unwanted computers and electronic devices. Freecycle (*www.freecycle.org*) is a worldwide organization comprised of groups of people in local communities. Their objective is to reduce waste by encouraging people to give away for free their unwanted items to people in their local communities who can use them. You can probably find someone in a Freecycle group who can use that computer or cell phone you no longer need.

Buying products that are recycling friendly is another way to reduce e-waste. Green computing products use more renewable materials, such as bamboo, instead of non-biodegradable plastics. The [re]drive Turbo USB 2.0 External Hard Drive from Simple Tech (see Figure 2.8) uses bamboo, which is biodegradable and fast growing, and aluminum—easily recyclable—to create an environmentally friendly product. Web sites such as The Green Lounge (*www.thegreenlounge.org*) can keep you abreast of trends in green computing.

Figure 2.8
Bamboo and aluminum components help make this hard drive environmentally friendly.

Recycling e-waste safely is the final step you can take. Many computer manufacturers sponsor their own computer recycling programs (see Figure 2.9). You can locate local recycling centers in your area by exploring sites such as Earth 911 (*http://earth911.org/*).

Figure 2.9
Many computer companies provide guidance on recycling and donation of unwanted computers in a number of different countries including the United States. If companies export wastes overseas for recycling or disposal, they have an ethical responsibility to train workers to recycle and reclaim materials in an environmentally friendly manner that minimizes worker exposure to toxic substances.

Keeping e-waste to a minimum and disposing of it safely is obviously good for the environment and society. By disposing of e-waste safely or recycling it in your own country, you are behaving ethically by treating residents of developing countries with respect instead of exploiting them.

Objective 6
Describe Web-Content Filtering and Its Effect on Free Speech

If you are an adult surfing the Web from home in the United States, you probably won't have trouble accessing sites on the Web and finding information on almost any topic you want. But what if you are restricted from seeing certain content on the Web "for your protection" or "for your own good"? Think this can't happen? It happens every day in the United States and many other countries and is a constant subject of ethical controversy. As usual, whether you find this practice to be ethical or unethical is a matter of personal opinion.

What is Web content filtering? *Web content filtering* means using software to restrict the availability of information that someone can find while surfing the Web. There are two main situations in which Web content filtering is used:

- **Politically**—Certain governments, such as China, want to restrict the availability of opposing political views and other sensitive information from their citizens.

- **Protectively**—The objective is to protect a certain group of people from objectionable, inappropriate, or offensive content, such as not allowing children access to pornography.

What type of political content filtering takes place? Many countries restrict access to information, but China is one of the most active. China has passed numerous laws regarding censorship, and state-owned ISPs block Web sites with content that violates these laws. The Golden Shield Project, often referred to as the Great Firewall of China, is a government network of firewalls and Internet servers that block specific URLs from being accessed. Web sites that are blocked include, but are not limited to, the following topics:

- Pornography or obscenity
- References to outlawed groups such as Falun Gong
- Commentaries on free speech, democracy, or Marxism
- Descriptions or photographs of Tiananmen Square protests of 1989 or other more recent protests
- Discussions of the Dalai Lama, his teachings, or the International Tibet Independence Movement

China employs an Internet police force to enforce their Internet laws. Comments on blogs or other discussion sites that are deemed to violate these laws are often rapidly deleted. In 2006, Google came under fire by many international civil rights groups when it agreed to deploy a version of their search engine for China that was self-censored by Google to meet the Chinese guidelines. The civil rights groups argued that Google was facilitating the suppression of free speech by the Chinese government. Google merely contended that it was complying with Chinese laws in an effort to provide search services to the Chinese people. The issue is still furiously debated today.

Why do people feel content needs to be filtered to protect individuals? Most people would agree that protecting children from pornography is an admirable objective. Controlling content placed on the Internet is difficult, especially in America and other countries where free speech is a right. Laws designed to restrict Internet content are often not passed due to concerns about the violation of the right to free speech. Therefore, since almost anything can be placed on the Internet, filtering content is one of the few options available. Schools and libraries in the United States are required to have filtering software on their computers to qualify for certain types of federal funding. Filtering software, like Net Nanny (see Figure 2.10) can be configured to block various categories of objectionable material.

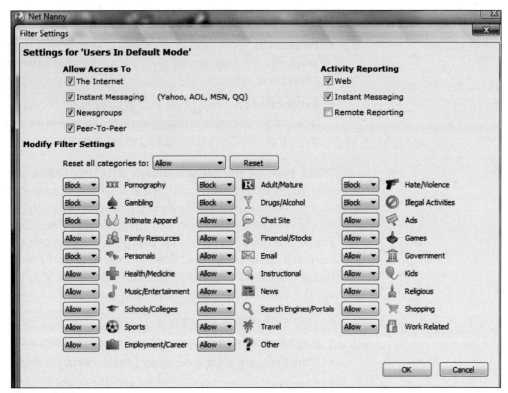

Figure 2.10
Net Nanny filtering software provides a wide range of content-blocking options.

Why is content filtering an ethical issue? Opponents of filtering software contend that when objectionable material—defined by arbitrary standards—is blocked, the infringement of free speech rights occurs. Actually, individuals are not prevented from exercising their right of free speech. But, infringing upon the rights of free access to information has generally been defined by the U.S. courts as a First Amendment (free speech) issue. Restricting free speech is not only illegal in the United States, but is also considered unethical. Supporters of content filtering contend that there are groups of people, like children, that need to be protected from objectionable material "for their own good" and that it would be unethical not to protect them.

But free speech is not necessarily a right of individuals in other countries. Although in the United States, we consider the restriction of free speech to be illegal, it is legal in many instances under Chinese law. So although you might consider the restriction of content to be unethical, the Chinese government has a different view. You need to consider ethical issues in the context of individual societies. In the case of free speech, for example, what is ethical in one country may be considered unethical in another.

Does content filtering actually protect people from objectionable content? In many instances, filtering software is effective. However, problems arise when the software is unable to discern between objectionable content and informational content. Content filtering software often looks for key words or phrases when determining whether or not to block a Web site. Sites that provide information on safe sex, support gay rights, or with information on breast cancer may be blocked because key-term filters might confuse them with pornographic sites. Sometimes the owners of pornography sites are adept at disguising the content of their sites in ways that fool the filtering software.

Because regulating the content of the Internet is not practical, content filtering remains one of the few options. Therefore, the debate over violating the rights of free speech—usually considered unethical—will rage on for the foreseeable future.

Objective 7
Define the Digital Divide and Describe Methods for Bridging It

Computers, the Internet, and other advanced technologies are becoming ubiquitous in the United States. Even the simple acts of ordering a sandwich at a local convenience store or running a gasoline pump often involve using touch screen computers. When you are doing research assignments for school—perhaps related to this book—the first resource you utilize is often the Internet. But what if you didn't have Internet access? What if you didn't even have access to a computer? What if you were unable to get clean drinking water because computer-controlled water purification systems were too expensive for your village to afford? Just like millions of other people around the world, in these instances you would find yourself on the wrong side of the digital divide.

What is the digital divide? The concept of a *digital divide* refers to the perceived gap between those people who have access to digital technology and those who do not. Although the term came into popular usage in 1996 after President Clinton and Vice President Gore began using the term in speeches, the concept of a division between haves and have-nots is hardly new. In the 1960s, Dr. Martin Luther King was one of the first social activists to recognize and articulate this problem in several speeches that he made. Dr. King said, "Modern man through scientific genius has been able to dwarf distance. Through our genius we have made this world a neighborhood. And yet we have not yet had the ethical commitment to make of it a brotherhood. But somehow, and in some way, we have got to do this." And these statements were made almost 20 years before the invention and popularization of the personal computer and 30 years before the widespread popularity of the Internet! Dr. King recognized that without equal access to technology, people might find themselves at a disadvantage.

Why is the digital divide an ethical issue? If you recall our discussion of ethics in Chapter 1, a key component of judging whether behavior is ethical is fairness. If certain groups are denied access to technology, they are put at an unfair disadvantage compared to those with access to the technology. And equal access to technology doesn't just mean computers. Many technologies contribute to improved quality of life such as new farming techniques, water purification equipment, transportation systems, and digital access to government services. Improving the quality of life of individuals tends to benefit society as a whole and therefore makes it a laudable ethical goal.

So we just need to give cheap computers to poor people to conquer the digital divide? If only it were that simple. The digital divide is not just about socioeconomic differences (poor versus rich). The divide also can be generational (youth versus senior citizens), geographic (urban versus rural . . . especially with Internet connectivity), or ethnic (racial). The gap in the digital divide is complex and is not as simple as throwing money at the problem to make it go away. First we need to consider the nuances that make up the gap.

What comprises the "gap" in the digital divide? There are two main components to the digital divide. The first is *physical access gap* which involves individuals who do not have ready access to technology (such as home PCs, the Internet, etc.) or when technology that is available elsewhere is not being used to effectively improve their lives. Do you have access to computer equipment? Is digital technology (such as kiosks to access government services) being used to improve the quality of your life? Do you posses a broadband Internet connection? Can you even get broadband access in the area where you live? Yes, having a dial-up connection to the Internet actually can put you on the wrong side of the digital divide because so much of the multimedia experience of the Internet today is dependent upon fast access speed. Many people only consider the physical access gap when considering the digital divide, but equally as important is the accessibility gap.

The *accessibility gap* refers mainly to the lack the knowledge (or varying degrees of knowledge) to use technology effectively (lack of computer literacy skills). Giving someone a computer without teaching them how to use it is of dubious value ... especially if they have never seen a computer before! Remember the first time you went on the Internet? Unless someone showed you what to do and where to start (such as how to use a Web browser), you probably struggled at first. But the accessibility gap also refers to physical limitations that prevent people from adequately accessing technology (such as the elderly and people with disabilities). To close the digital divide, physical access and accessibility issues must both be addressed.

Has the availability of inexpensive computers in the U.S. effectively eliminated the physical access gap? True, computers are relatively inexpensive in the U.S. But that still doesn't mean everyone can afford to own one. In many countries such as China and India, computers are still unaffordable to a large percentage of the population. Also, if you don't have a computer in your home, you are forced to rely on shared-access computers at your job, your school, the public library, or Internet cafes. And don't forget, the cost of accessing technology isn't limited to the cost of a computer and monitor.

If you actually want to do something with the computer, you are going to need software. Yes, there are free software programs available, but you may need to purchase a product like Microsoft Office to maintain compatibility with coworkers. And access to the Internet isn't free. While dial-up connections can still be relatively cheap, their slow speed will make your Internet experience rather inefficient or downright painful in many instances. Broadband connections cost $30 a month and up, which isn't necessarily in everyone's budget. And backup hardware and software and networking equipment is an additional expense if you are planning on establishing connectivity between multiple computers (or sharing Internet access). The cost of computing still presents a physical barrier for many individuals in the United States and other countries.

Won't the accessibility gap close on its own as computers become more user-friendly? This is a position that is popular in certain circles. Certainly, computers are becoming more user-friendly. That helps many people caught in the accessibility gap, but not all—don't forget about the physical gap! Children are exposed to technology at a much earlier age and use it on a regular basis. Many people equate the comfort level that today's generation has with technology with proficiency. Unfortunately, growing up with technology doesn't necessarily guarantee computer literacy. You still need to know how to use the technology effectively and efficiently. Being connected to the Internet or having an easy to use point-and-click interface doesn't help you if you don't know where to look for information or how to interpret what you find.

How do we close the digital divide? There are many organizations that are working on solutions, and you can start by getting involved or supporting them. Start by finding organizations in your community that provide computer access and training to underserved populations. Your local library, community college, community center, or social service organizations are great places to begin.

One of the most famous organizations working on closing the digital divide is The One Laptop Per Child Association, Inc. (*http://laptop.org*). OLPC is an organization funded by major corporations such as AMD, eBay, Google, and Red Hat with the goal of providing affordable laptops to children in developing countries. Individuals also provide support mostly by funding the purchase of individual computers for donation. The XO-1 laptop (see Figure 2.11) is a sturdy computer with flash memory instead of a hard drive that runs on a version of the Linux operating system. It features networking capabilities to foster working on shared projects by users and to enable many computers to access a single Internet connection. The specially designed graphical user interface called Sugar was designed to make collaboration easy for novice users. Millions of laptops have already been purchased by a number of developing countries.

Figure 2.11
The XO laptop is designed to provide an inexpensive computing solution for the masses in developing countries.

Other less well known organizations, such as EduVision, Inveneo, and Geekcorps (*www.geekcorps.org*), are working on various hardware, infrastructure, and training projects to shrink the digital divide. Geekcorps (see Figure 2.12) recruits technology professionals to work in various parts of the world with local partners to design and deploy communication infrastructure and to teach technology in small group settings. If you have the appropriate technology experience, you can volunteer to work for Geekcorps and possibly go overseas when participating in projects. But Geekcorps makes it easy for everyone to support them by doing something that many people already do on a regular basis—buy merchandise from Amazon.com. Following the link to Amazon on Geekcorps, Web site results in commissions to Geekcorps for all purchases you make in that visit to Amazon. So while the digital divide isn't going to be closed overnight, you can get involved and help shrink the divide in your part of the global community.

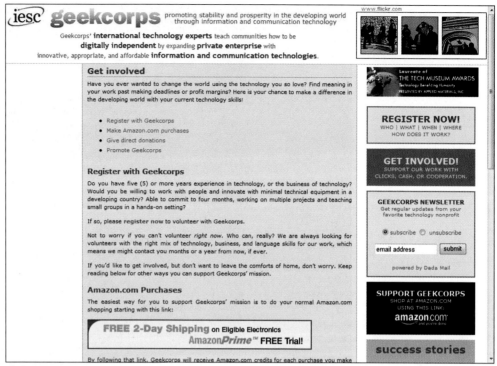

Figure 2.12
You can provide support to organizations such as Geekcorps and start bridging the digital divide.

Objective 8
Describe Methods to Evaluate the Accuracy of Digital Information

You can find almost anything on the Internet just by using a search engine such as Google or Yahoo. Everyone seems to receive helpful e-mails from friends and family warning you about a variety of issues, such as the police in your state giving out speeding tickets. Because anyone can put up a Web page on any subject imaginable or send off a quick e-mail, how can you distinguish fact from fiction? Determining the reliability of information you encounter in cyberspace can be a challenge. It is also critically important when you use the Web as a source of scholarly research. Your biology professor would probably give you a poor grade if you presented her with a research paper on the rare Pacific Northwest Tree Octopus (see Figure 2.13).

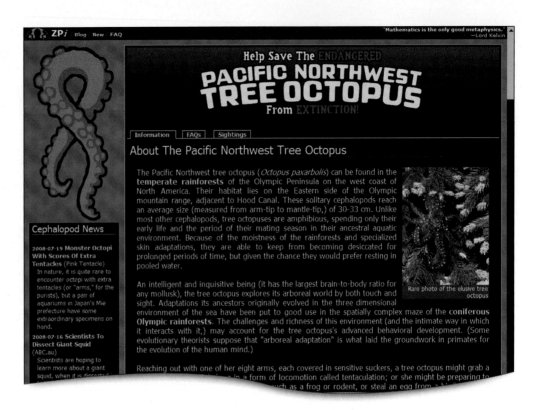

Figure 2.13
A joke Web site that looks real if you don't know that an octopus lives only in the ocean!

Is posting false information on the Internet unethical? Most people would agree that posting false information is unethical; however, that doesn't stop people from posting blatantly false or erroneous information on the Web because of the ease with which you can disseminate information on the Internet and often remain anonymous. In less than an hour, someone can create a credible looking Web site that presents "evidence" to support the premise that the 1906 San Francisco earthquake never took place. But given the overwhelming amount of historical evidence—including still photos and newspaper interviews with earthquake survivors—you know that a devastating earthquake did occur in California in 1906. Not only is trying to change history by lying unethical, but it is disrespectful to the memories of the people who suffered through a catastrophic event like an earthquake.

Why would someone disseminate false information? Certain Web sites portray facts in a distorted fashion to support an organization's point. The dissemination of false or distorted information is often used to further an agenda of hate speech, racism, or the perpetuation of stereotypes. Bogus or exaggerated claims are made to sell ineffective products, such as "miracle weight loss drugs." Organizations might distort facts, make sweeping generalizations, or state opinions as facts to support fund-raising campaigns, especially for causes that have an emotional component, such as cruelty to animals or impoverished people. Other individuals enjoy seeing how many people they can fool into believing information that is false.

Unfortunately, many inaccuracies on the Internet are unintentional. People writing content for Web pages may not check their facts to ensure they are accurate. Others perpetuate bad information by using an erroneous source of information and then using those facts to generate new Internet content for other Web sites. Obviously, if you are going to rely on information from a Web site—especially if you are doing scholarly research—you need to take steps to ensure that the information is accurate and the site is appropriate for your needs.

There are many instances of intentional misrepresentations on the Internet. Some Web sites, such as the Tree Octopus, or the last Web page (see Figure 2.14) are obvious attempts at humor or parodies of other legitimate Web sites. Because it sometimes can be difficult to tell fact from fiction on the Internet, you need a strategy for evaluating what you will encounter while surfing the Web.

Figure 2.14
An obvious joke because there is no last page to the Internet.

What criteria should you use for evaluating the suitability of a Web site? Evaluation criteria are similar to those you use for printed resources that you would find in your school library. You need to consider the following:

- **Who is the author?**—Is information about the author —including contact information—readily available on the site? If you know the author's name, you can search the Internet or other resources to consider the expertise of the author. Is the author a noted leader in the field he is writing about and recognized as an authority by others you respect? Does the author have appropriate credentials such as college degrees or relevant work experience that gives you comfort to know he has expertise in the field? Although you might find what you consider to be good information on an anonymous blogger's Web site, you don't have any information about the blogger to consider him an authority on a subject.

- **Who is the publisher of the information or the owner of the Web site?** —Is the organization that owns or sponsors the Web site clearly identified? Is that entity an appropriate source of information for the topic you are researching? Is the publisher respected in the field and relied upon by others? Obviously, a respected journalistic body like the New York Times (*www.nytimes.com*) has more credibility than Billy Bob's Bodacious Blog!

  Carefully examine the URL for the Web site for clues. Domains—the portion of the web address after the dot—are often set up for specific purposes: *.gov* and *.mil* are for government and military entities, *.edu* is for educational institutions, and *.org* is mostly for non-profit organizations, although other entities can get *.org* addresses now. For instance, URLs for personal Web sites or less well known businesses need more scrutiny than a Web site like *www.irs.gov* when seeking tax advice. Educational entities (*.edu*) may have more scholarly credibility than Web sites in the *.com* domain, in which anyone can register a site.

- **What is the relationship of the author to the publisher?**—Is the author an employee of the publishing entity? Or, does the author have a more casual relationship with the publisher such as generating content for a fee? Employees *might* be held to a more stringent level of competence and be required to have more appropriate credentials than independent contractors.

- **The point of view or bias**—Writers tend to use information that helps them make their points to the reader. A good writer is objective and provides different points of view, even when they are detrimental to his argument. The writer should also acknowledge when he is presenting his opinion as opposed to facts, and controversial theories should be identified as such.

  Consider the organization and how it might be affected by the information. If you are reviewing information about products that the company publishing the Web site sells, be aware that the information presented may be intended to persuade people to buy the product. Corporate Web sites tend to paint the corporation in the most positive light, whereas a site not sponsored by the corporation might provide a more objective opinion about the company's operations and products. Also consider whether the publisher has a particular political, religious, or philosophical agenda that may encourage him to slant the information that is presented to support their causes.

- **Does the work cite sources?**—Just as your professors expect you to use footnotes and a bibliography in your research papers, scholarly publications on the Internet should also list their sources of information. When presented with a list of sources, check them. Are the sources respected publications or from authoritative and reliable authors on other Web sites?

- **Is the accuracy of the work verifiable?**—Can you find the sources listed in the bibliography? Do hyperlinks to other articles work so you can review the sources? For articles involving research, were the research methods, the data collected, and the interpretation of the results provided so that the research study could be reproduced if necessary?

- **Is the information presented current?**—Are dates of publication clearly indicated on the Web site? When the work is updated, are updates clearly identified and dated? Are the dates at which research information was gathered presented (for example, "based on a study conducted by XYZ Consultants in May, 2011")?

Finally, after following these steps, take a step back and consider what you have found. Decide why the page was placed on the Web. Was the main goal of the page to inform, persuade, or sell? Consider whether the page was intended to be a parody or a satire. The best indicator for this is the tone of the writing. Was the writer sarcastic? Did he tend to use a lot of humor or exaggerate to make points? Was the page supplemented with outlandish or humorous photographs? Decide if there are better places to find your needed research than on the Internet. Are the Web sites you are evaluating as credible as respected published periodicals or texts that you would consult in your college library? If after all of this analysis you feel comfortable, then you might have found a good source of reliable information on the Web.

Can I rely on the information I find in Wikipedia? Because anyone can add content to Wikipedia, the world's largest online encyclopedia, many people wonder if it is a reliable source of information. Wikipedia entries are reviewed by editors so there is some control over the accuracy of content. But just as any other source of information, articles in Wikipedia need to be evaluated based on the criteria described previously. Recent studies have shown that Wikipedia, for science and nature articles, contain about the same number of errors as the *Encyclopædia Britannica*. Many articles on Wikipedia have extensive footnotes and lists of sources so you can investigate the reliability of the source material. So treat Wikipedia as you would any other Web page upon which you might want to rely; evaluate it thoroughly before relying on it.

Is there a resource for finding quality sites for scholarly research? There are several resources on the Internet, most of which were created by librarians, that can be useful for quickly locating Web sites that are considered reliable, current, and suitable for academic research. Some of the more popular ones are the Librarian's Internet Index, The Internet Public Library, Infomine, and Academic Info. These are described in the table in Figure 2.15.

Web Site Name	Description	Web Site Address
Librarian's Internet Index	Publically funded Web site maintained by librarians that finds and evaluates high quality information sites. Currently has links to over 20,000 resources.	*www.lii.org*
INFOMINE	Built and maintained by librarians, INFOMINE focuses on resources relevant to university-level faculty, students, and research staff. Resources listed include databases, electronic journals, electronic books, articles, and directories of researchers.	*http://infomine.ucr.edu*
The Internet Public Library	Another librarian constructed information resource that strives to provide links to resources that have been evaluated by librarians and determined to contain high quality information. The IPL also serves as a research forum and an online test bed for new information technologies	*www.ipl.org*

Figure 2.15
Resources for finding quality Web sites.

The Librarian's Internet Index (see Figure 2.16) is easy to use as it closely resembles other search engines and subject directories. But, the pages indexed in LII have been carefully reviewed for accuracy and currency by librarians and other scholars who maintain the site. This doesn't mean you don't have to check facts, but it does provide you with an excellent starting point for your research.

Type in key terms to use the search engine feature.

Browse through evaluated Web pages by subject.

Figure 2.16
The Librarian's Internet Index can be used like a conventional search engine or you can browse through it by subject.

Following these guidelines should ensure that you are relying on accurate information for your research needs. There is one more category of false information that requires some additional measures to handle, and that is e-mail hoaxes.

What is a hoax? A *hoax* is anything that is designed to deceive another person either as a practical joke or for financial gain. It attempts to make someone believe something that is untrue. Hoaxes perpetrated in cyberspace that are designed to part suckers from their money are classified as cybercrimes. Cybercrime hoaxes generally target a single individual. In this section, you will explore hoaxes that target a large audience and are generally perpetrated as practical jokes, agents of social change (poking fun at the established norm in an effort to change it), or a waste people's valuable time. Although there are hoax Web sites, most cyberspace hoaxes are perpetrated by e-mail.

Why do people create e-mail hoaxes? As opposed to garnering financial rewards, the motives of e-mail hoax creators can be more complex. Many people start e-mail hoaxes just for the challenge of seeing if their "brainchild" can be spread globally. Other hoaxes start as innocent practical jokes between friends, but then take on a life of their own via the fast communication on the Internet. Many hoaxes become so well known that they are incorporated into society as true events even though they are false. Once this happens, they are known as ***urban legends***. An example of an urban legend is the story about a man who wakes up in a bathtub full of ice water to discover he has had his kidney taken out. Hoaxes are similar to acts of real world vandalism such as graffiti. Just as graffiti artists "make their mark on the world" hoaxers may consider they are making a similar mark when a bogus e-mail they created becomes widespread.

Sometimes hoaxes are based on misinformation or the venting of frustration. An e-mail hoax that reappears every time there is a spike in gasoline prices is the Gas Boycott, or Gas War hoax (see Figure 2.17). The e-mail touts the scheme as being invented by reputable businessmen to boost its credibility. The e-mail explains how boycotting certain gasoline companies will drive the price of gasoline down and urges recipients of the e-mail to join the fight. The originator of this hoax was probably frustrated by high gas prices and had a poor understanding of economics. Unfortunately, this tactic will have no effect on gasoline prices as it only shifts demand for gasoline from certain oil companies to other sources. Because it does not reduce the overall demand for gasoline, the price of gas will not decline. How many of you received this e-mail and thought it sounded like plausible idea?

Figure 2.17
The Gas War hoax is a typical e-mail hoax.

How can I tell if an e-mail is a hoax? Sometimes it is difficult to separate fact from fiction. Many hoax e-mails are well written and crafted in such a way that they sound real. Before hitting the Forward button and sending an e-mail to all your friends, first check it out at one of the many Web sites that keep track of e-mail hoaxes and expose them. Check sites such as *www.snopes.com, www.hoax-slayer.com* (see Figure 2.18), or *www.truthorfiction.com.* These sites are searchable, so you can enter a few key words from the e-mail you suspect may be a hoax and quickly find similar e-mails with an explanation of whether they are true or false.

Checking out e-mails before forwarding them on to friends, family, and coworkers will save other people's time and help end the spread of these time wasters.

Get alerts to new hoaxes by subscribing

Use keywords from a suspected e-mail to find similar hoaxes

Browse hoaxes by category

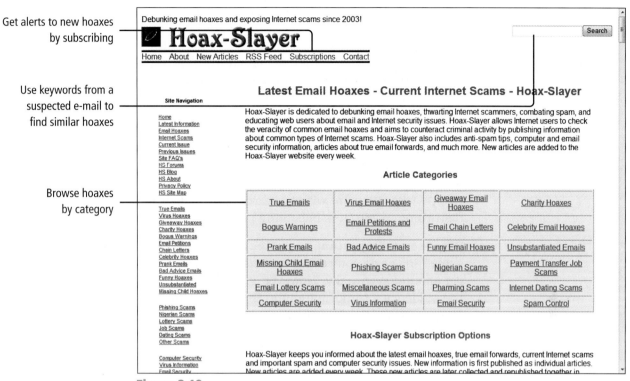

Figure 2.18
Hoax-Slayer.com is a useful resource for researching suspected hoaxes.

Not passing on information that is false is all part of being an ethical Internet user. It takes more effort on your part to check potential hoaxes, but think of all the time you'll save your friends and family by not sending out endless streams of hoax e-mails!

Objective 9
Define Online Reputation and Describe Methods for Protecting Your Online Reputation

There may already be quite a bit of information about you on the Internet. Chances are you've put quite a bit of it out there yourself possibly through social networking sites such as MySpace, Facebook, and LinkedIn. Most people strive to maintain a good reputation in the real world because this helps them get good jobs, make friends, develop business relationships, and generally makes life easier to conduct. But in the twenty-first century, your online, virtual reputation is just as important as your real-life one.

What exactly is my online reputation? Your *online reputation* is an extension of your real-life reputation. Your real-life reputation is the view held by the community, the general public, friends, family, and coworkers of your general character. Are you considered an honest person? Do you always speak your mind regardless of the consequences? Are you known for defending the rights of less fortunate individuals? These are examples of factors that contribute to society's view of the type of individual you are.

Your online reputation consists of the information that is available about you in cyberspace that can influence people in the real world regarding your character. Information is constantly added to the Internet about many of us, even by people we don't know. It can be challenging to control the information that contributes to your online reputation. If you go to a party this weekend and some of the guests take pictures of you or videos at the party, these people may post their media to Flickr or YouTube and identify—known as **tagging**—you in the pictures and video. Your friends might be writing about you on their MySpace pages as you read this. Perhaps someone you work with is talking about you on his or her blog. Even if what they are writing is true, false, misleading, embarrassing, or disturbing to you, it is becoming part of your online reputation.

Why is it so important to protect my online reputation? If you say something or do something you wish you hadn't in real life, people will forget about it eventually. However, given the *persistence of information*—the tendency for information on the Internet to remain on the Internet for long periods of time—pictures, videos, and narratives about you might never disappear. Even if you delete something, it probably still exists somewhere. Sites such as the Internet Archive—*www.archive.org*—feature utilities such as the Wayback Machine that can show you what a Web site looked like at a previous point in time. Ever wonder what Yahoo looked like way back in the dark ages, such as in 1996, of the Internet? A search

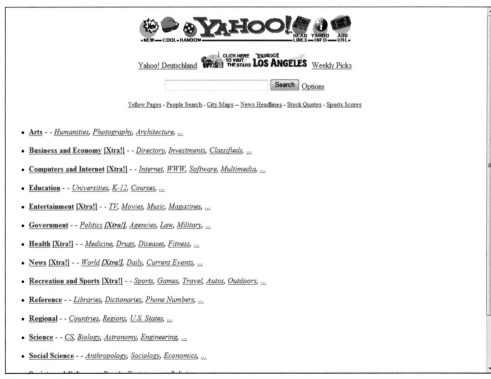

Figure 2.19
A much simpler Yahoo home page is preserved for posterity in the Internet Archive. Your Web pages might live on forever also.

on the Wayback Machine shows you that it looked like Figure 2.19. Cyberspace has a much longer memory than humans. When reputation was spread only by word of mouth, it tended to encompass a small area. Now, you can move halfway around the world, and negative information about you is much more easily discovered.

Of course your reputation varies depending on who is interpreting the cyberspace information about you. You friends might be impressed by that picture on MySpace of you doing a headstand on your skateboard. Your mother is less likely to be impressed when she spots it and worries that you might get seriously injured by your tricks.

What are the ethical issues surrounding my online reputation? The main ethical issues are truthfulness and fairness. Does your online reputation portray accurately, or truthfully, the type of person you are? Would all third parties researching you on the Internet arrive at the correct conclusion about your nature and character based on the available information, or fairness related to that availability of information?

Obviously, you don't want your friends, family, or coworkers to post inaccurate or misleading information about you online that would portray your character in an inappropriate manner to others. Conversely, you shouldn't act unethically yourself by posting false information on the Internet in an attempt to artificially enhance your reputation.

Why should I care what others think of my online reputation? According to the University of Massachusetts Center for Market research, 54 percent of college admissions officers research candidates on the Internet. Employers also routinely browse through social networking sites (such as MySpace and Facebook) and blogs to evaluate job applicants as part of making hiring decisions. And even after you are hired, if your employer finds things that it doesn't like on one of your sites you might be fired because of it. In early 2008, CNN producer Chez Pazienza alleged he was discharged by CNN because it felt he had violated CNN journalism standards on a personal blog that he writes called Deus Ex Malcontent. The most famous firing for blogging was also the first instance of this practice. Ellen Simonetti was a Delta Airlines flight attendant who was fired by Delta because the company objected to pictures that she posted on her blog.

How can an employer fire me for writing something on my own time? Don't we have free speech in the United States? Yes, you do have a constitutional right to free speech. However, that doesn't mean your employer is going to agree with your opinions. In the majority of the states, the *employment at-will* principle governs the firing of employees. Employment at-will means that unless you are covered by an employment contract or a collective bargaining agreement, such as a union contract, employers can fire you at any time for any reason, unless the reason violates a legal statute such as race discrimination. You employer is not required to provide you with a reason for the firing, but can simply tell you not to report for work any longer. Therefore, it is a good idea to be aware of the attitudes and behaviors that your employer might find objectionable and steer clear of those issues on sites where you are easily identifiable (see Figure 2.20).

Besides losing my job, what other problems can a bad online reputation cause me? It could perhaps get you put in jail! Consider Joshua

Lipton who was arrested for a drunken driving accident in which another person was seriously injured. When the case came to trial, the prosecutor presented a picture of Lipton taken two weeks after the accident when he was attending a Halloween party. He was dressed as a prisoner in an orange jumpsuit labeled *Jail bird*. The prosecutor successfully argued that Lipton was not repentant over his actions, but was instead joking about them. Lipton was sentenced to two years in prison. The prosecutor had found the picture on a Facebook page from someone who attended the party.

Figure 2.20
Pictures posted on social networking sites can be used to defend or defame your character depending upon the context.

Can I take legal action against someone who damages my reputation? You can try. In this case, you would be filing a ***defamation*** suit—also called libel or slander suit. Defamation results when a false claim is made that portrays an individual, group, business, or product in a negative light, thereby damaging the reputation. ***Libel*** is defamation in written or visual depictions, and most cyberspace defamation suits revolve around libel. ***Slander*** usually relates to verbal statements and gestures; it is a more common source of legal action in the real world. Unfortunately, many defamation suits filed over statements made in cyberspace are dismissed by judges based on first amendment, free speech grounds. However, certain cases involving serious damage to reputations do make it all the way through to a trial.

What steps should I take to protect my online reputation? Exercise care in putting personal details about yourself on the Internet. Make sure there is a compelling reason to reveal information before doing so. Be vigilant about the access you grant to social networking sites. Make your profiles visible only to friends. Be selective about the friends you connect with on these sites. You need to be satisfied that they are people you can trust and not just casual acquaintances or friends of friends. If you are blogging, consider remaining anonymous.

You need to examine your own reputation periodically. Google yourself and see what information about you is available on the Web. If you see something that displeases you, ask the poster or the webmaster to remove the offending material. Don't have time to constantly monitor your reputation? Products such as MyReputation (see Figure 2.21) and Trackur provide automatic searches and updates regarding information posted about you online.

Figure 2.21
MyReputation from Reputation Defender provides comprehensive reports about the information about you that is on the Web and provides you with assistance in having the information removed.

Keeping your online reputation accurate and not unfairly damaging other people's cyberspace reputations is an integral part of being an ethical cyber-citizen.

Summary

Engaging in ethical behavior on the Internet means you will exercise common sense and good judgment. Stop and think before you act to consider the ramifications of your actions and their effects on other individuals.

- Do you really want to pass on that unsubstantiated rumor about a classmate on your Facebook page?

- How would you feel if someone posted an embarrassing picture of you on the Internet?

- Is saving a little time on an English class assignment worth potentially failing the course and being kicked out of school because you copied the information for the paper directly from a Web site?

- Do you really want representatives from a federal law enforcement agency coming to your house, seizing your computer and leveling massive finds on you just because you wanted to save a few bucks and illegally download a copy of the movie *Spiderman 3*?

- If the band you were in recorded a cool new song would you want people swapping MP3 files of it on the Internet while you received no compensation for your hard work?

- Do you really need a new computer, or can you make your current one last another year and thereby avoid having it tossed into a landfill in India?

Being an ethical citizen in cyberspace takes extra time and effort. But the rewards of treating others fairly and with respect are worth it.

Key Terms

Accessibility gap	76	Hoax	85	Phishing	63
Cyberbullying	60	Identity theft	65	Physical access gap	76
Cybercrimes	62	Industrial espionage	56	Privacy	53
Cyber-harrassment	60	Invasion of Privacy	53	Slander	90
Cyberloafing	56	Keystroke loggers	58	Social engineering	63
Cyberstalking	60	Libel	90	Tagging	88
Defamation	90	Online reputation	87	Urban legends	85
Digital divide	75	Persistence of information	88	Web content filtering	73
Employment at-will	89				
E-waste	70	Pretexting	63	White collar crime	56

End-of-Chapter Assessments

Matching

Match each term in the second column with its correct definition in the first column by writing the letter of the term on the blank line in front of the correct definition.

_____ **1.** The perceived gap between those with access to technology and those without access.

_____ **2.** Using a created scenario (usually over the phone) to trick an individual into revealing sensitive information.

_____ **3.** The tendency for information to endure.

_____ **4.** The right to be left alone to do as one pleases.

_____ **5.** Using the Internet to avoid working.

_____ **6.** Preventing access to objectionable material on the Web.

_____ **7.** An attempt to trick people into revealing sensitive information usually through the use of e-mail or another means.

_____ **8.** An attempt to trick someone into believing false information.

_____ **9.** Using the Internet to harass a classmate.

_____ **10.** Not having ready access to technology.

A Cyberbullying

B Cyberloafing

C Digital divide

D Hoax

E Persistence of information

F Phishing

G Physical access gap

H Pretexting

I Privacy

J Web content filtering

Fill in the Blank

Write the correct answer in the space provided.

1. The _____ refers to people who lack the necessary skills to use a particular technology.

2. Software programs that keep track of all input via a computer keyboard are known as _____.

3. _____ is a false oral statement about an individual.

4. False information that becomes stories or facts that many people believe are known as _____.

5. _____ occurs when someone's personal privacy has been violated.

6. Playing an online game instead of working at your job is an example of _____.

7. The right of an employer to fire you at any time for any reason is known as the _____ doctrine.

8. Impersonating someone with the intent to defraud another institution, such as a credit card company, is called _____.

9. The tendency for information to remain somewhere in cyberspace for long periods of time—perhaps forever—is known as _____.

10. Personal information about you that is available in cyberspace and enables others to draw conclusions about the type of person you are is known as your _____.

11. False claims that are made about an individual that damages his reputation is collectively known as _____.

12. Written or visual depictions of defamation are known as _____.

13. A form of _____ is using a fake e-mail account to bombard a classmate with rude and insulting messages.

14. _____ software is often used to prevent children from accessing pornography sites.

15. Poor people in the United States who are unable to afford a computer or Internet access are said to be on the wrong side of the _____.

End-of-Chapter Assessments

Multiple Choice

Circle the letter of the item that correctly answers the question.

1. The "digital divide":
   a. Is impossible to close
   b. Can be closed by providing individuals with inexpensive computers
   c. Requires ongoing community effort to bring technology resources to underserved populations
   d. Deals only with access to the Internet

2. Monitoring an employee's Internet use by an employer is:
   a. Illegal in the United States
   b. Legal in most areas of the United States
   c. Legal only if the employee is informed about the monitoring
   d. Legal only in Florida, California, Nevada, and New Jersey

3. Web content filtering is said to breach an individual's right to:
   a. Privacy
   b. Free information
   c. Self awareness
   d. Free speech

4. When many people believe a false story and the story becomes almost a universally accepted anecdote, the story is said to have become:
   a. An urban legend
   b. Folklore
   c. Wisdom
   d. An Internet reality tale

5. The right to privacy for Americans is:
   a. Specifically granted in the Fourth Amendment of the Constitution
   b. Granted by section 7 of the Bill of Rights
   c. Alluded to in the Fourth Amendment of the Constitution and interpreted by the courts as a right
   d. A key component of the Declaration of Independence

6. The two main reasons employers monitor employees are:
   a. Prevention of theft and measurement of productivity
   b. Prevention of theft and amusement
   c. Measurement of productivity and exercise of strict control of the workforce
   d. Provide laughs at the Christmas party and blackmail

(Multiple Choice—continues on the next page)

Multiple Choice

(Multiple Choice–continued)

7. All of the following are types of cyberbullies except:
   a. The Vengeful Angel
   b. The Power Hungry
   c. Mean Girls
   d. Sneaky Meany

8. Which of the following statements about identity theft is *not* true?
   a. A significant percentage of identity theft occurs through methods other than online information theft.
   b. Identity theft incidents occur online over 90 percent of the time.
   c. Identity thieves can take out mortgages in the victim's name and then disappear with the cash.
   d. Freezing your credit history is an effective method for preventing identity theft.

9. An effective way to mitigate the problems related to e-waste is to:
   a. Use electronic products for as long as possible
   b. Donate products that you no longer need to other individuals
   c. Buy electronic products that contain easily recyclable components
   d. All of the above

10. Which of the following is *least* important when evaluating the quality of a Web site for research purposes?
   a. The reputation of the author in the field being written about
   b. The relationship of the author to the Web site publisher
   c. The links on the Web site to other sites covering the same topic
   d. Sources cited in the work are from credible publications

Outcome-Based Assessments

Apply the objectives in this chapter by answering the following questions:

1. Does your school use filtering software in computer labs on campus? If so, what types of Web sites are filtered? Who should decide what sites should be blocked by filtering software? The government? Librarians? Educators? Would you install filtering software on your home computer to protect your children? What types of sites would you block, and why would you block those sites?

2. How do you normally dispose of your used electronic equipment? Use the Internet to find recycling programs in your area that are designed to handle e-waste. Is there a cost involved for dropping off materials to be recycled? What Internet sites can you use to locate organizations in your area that take donations of used electronic equipment?

3. Have you ever been the target of a phishing scam? What information was the scammer trying to obtain from you? Was the scammer successful in soliciting information from you? How can you protect yourself from phishing scams in the future?

4. Research identity theft on the Internet. What is the average amount of dollars lost per incident? How much time does the average victim spend clearing up an identity theft problem? Does your state allow you to freeze your credit report and if so, what is the procedure you must follow to do so? Prepare a checklist for victims of identity theft that provide them with the steps they need to follow if they have become a victim.

5. Does your employer or your school monitor your computer usage? If you aren't sure, find out. What types of activities are prohibited under the acceptable use policy at your employer or school? Have you ever violated the terms of the acceptable use policy? If yes, were you caught? How effective do you think monitoring is in preventing wrongdoing?

6. Google yourself. How many references did you find that you didn't know about? Are any of these damaging to your online reputation? Is there anything on any Web sites where you maintain pages—MySpace, Facebook, and so on—that might be damaging to your reputation? Is there anything on your friends' sites that might portray you in a bad light? If an employer searched for information about you online, what impression of your character would they form?

7. Have you or one of your friends ever been the victim of a cyberbully? If so, what exactly happened and how did you handle it? What procedures do you think should be put in place at an elementary school to decrease the chances of cyberbullying occurring?

8. Using the Internet, research organizations are taking steps to bridge the digital divide. What organizations are operating in your community to solve this problem? What are the underserved populations—that is, the people without appropriate access to technology—in the county where your college is located? What programs do you think should be developed in the county to help these underserved populations gain more access to technology?

Index